HOCKEY'S YOUNG SUPERSTARS

ERIC DWYER

POLESTAR
BOOK PUBLISHERS

HOCKEY'S YOUNG SUPERSTARS

To my mother for her love and support and to the others
who've meant the most in my life, my wife Millie and son Eric Jr.

Published by:
Polestar Press Ltd.
P.O. Box 69382, Station K
Vancouver, B.C.   V5K 4W6

Distributed in Canada by:
Raincoast Book Distribution Ltd.
112 East Third Avenue
Vancouver, B.C.   V5T 1C8

This book has been published with the financial assistance
of the Canada Council and the
British Columbia Cultural Services Branch

Book and cover design by Jim Brennan
Production by Julian Ross and GoldRush Type & Graphics
Hockey card collage on page 120 by Eric Dwyer.
Cover photographs by Chris Relke
Interior photos by Chris Relke on pages 9, 11, 14, 17, 19,
32, 35, 37, 40, 43, 59, 60, 63, 64, 96, 94, 95 and 99.

Interior photos from Bruce Bennett Studios on pages 21, 22, 25, 27,
31, 47, 48, 51, 52, 55, 56, 67, 68, 71, 75, 76, 79, 81, 82, 85, 86, 89, 91,
101, 104, 106, 107, 108, 111, 112, 115, and 116.
These include photos by B. Bennett, M. DiGirolamo, J. Giamundo,
S. Levy, D. MacLellan, B. Winkler, and B. Wippert.

Printed in Canada

Canadian Cataloguing in Publication Data

Dwyer, Eric
Hockey's young superstars
ISBN 0-919591-92-2
I. Title.
GV848.5.A1D99 1992   796.962'092'2   092-090560-9

CONTENTS

Eric Dwyer

There's only one way to tell when a player has finally passed over the threshhold into stardom in the NHL. Don't waste your time checking the morning newspaper for scoring statistics. The real measure of stardom is not the number of goals or points they score, or the size of their contracts.

The real test comes every time kids gather on a snow-covered rink in Cape Breton or Saskatchewan. Or when they're scraping their sticks on a rainy driveway in Vancouver or in the slush in Toronto. Listen to the names that rise above the din, the players they impersonate in their mock play-by-play. Those pick-up Hockey Night in Canada games are as much a part of our heritage as frozen toes and missing teeth.

> Breathes there a Canadian with soul so dead,
> Who never to himself hath said:
> "Gretzky over to Kurri,
> He shoots, he scores!"

Times and hairstyles may change, but the pretend play-by-play has been a childhood constant ever since that first night when Foster Hewitt climbed into the gondola in Maple Leaf Gardens and uttered those immortal words, "Hello Canada and hockey fans in the United States." Strangely or perhaps characteristically, even from that first day, Canadian kids never used their own names in their running accounts of heroic rushes on the net and spectacular saves. It was always the name of the idols of the day—Clancy, Joliat, Apps, Richard, Howe, Hull, Beliveau, Orr, Lafleur, Gretzky, Lemieux.

INTRODUCTION

Listen on those long winter nights when kids dance the great childhood ballet, under a street light, around a couple of rocks pretending to be goalposts, and you will hear each move accompanied by a description stolen from Foster Hewitt, Danny Gallivan, Bob Cole or Jim Robson. Listen to the hub-bub as the players run and leap, each move etched by contrails of hot breath, and you'll hear the names of the real stars rise into the night. The greats are frozen forever in the crisp air, the one true Hockey Hall of Fame.

The game has been kind to each generation. With the natural conceit of youth we all describe our favourites as the best ever. The stars at night always seemed brighter when we were young. So did the stars on ice. In fact and statistic, each generation actually is a little better than the last.

We never thought we'd see another demon as possessed and driven as Rocket Richard. Until Bobby Clarke came along. There'd never be another centre as smooth and powerful as Jean Beliveau. And there wasn't until Mario Lemieux arrived. A Gretzky erases a Howe from the record book. A Bourque surpasses an Orr in fact if not in legend. A Hull begets a Hull. Hockey's evolution never ends.

Expansion was supposed to thin the herd and weaken the strain. But twenty-five years later it's stronger than ever. The old original six generated an interest in the game that spread worldwide. Now, like prodigal sons, those offsprings of hockey are returning to the NHL. Never has the league enjoyed such depth of young talent. The next generation of superstars has already hit the ice flying and scoring. Russians named Fedorov and Bure. Swedes named Sundin and Lidstrom. Czechs named Jagr and Holik. Americans named Leetch, Roenick and Modano. Even Irishmen named Nolan and Shanahan. And, of course, great new Canadian kids named Fleury, Sakic and Linden. They are the sons of Superseries '72.

It's impossible to overestimate the value that first showdown between the NHL and the Soviets played in the development of the latest generation of stars. Publicly, both sides claimed victory in 1972. Privately, they both knew better. The Canadians won more games. The Soviets won more respectability. They both realized they'd

have to work a lot harder if they didn't want to be embarrassed in future meetings. The Russians had to add physical and mental toughness to their game. Prior to '72, body contact in the Russian game was almost accidental, not intentional. The Canadians knew they were a couple of steps too slow to keep up with the rapidly-improving international game. They were sending Mack trucks out to race with sports cars.

There were some minor changes at the top but the real revolution took place at the bottom of the hockey pyramid in each country. In North America there was a change in emphasis so kids spent more time learning than playing during their early years. Twenty years later, that bottom of the pyramid has finally worked its way to the top. North American kids are finally as fast and skilled as Europeans. The Russians, Swedes, Czechs and Finns are finally as tough and competitive as the North Americans.

Harold Ballard once snorted in disgust that if one of his imports, Inge Hammarstrom, went into the corner with an egg in each pocket he'd come out without either one broken. Today, he'd come out with an omelette in each pocket.

Watch a videotape of the original six-team NHL and you'll think your VCR is stuck on slowmotion. Philadelphia's Broad Street Bullies wouldn't scare anybody today. You can't mug what you can't catch. They beat the Russians in the corners in the '70s—a plan Herb Brooks borrowed as the cornerstone of the Miracle On Ice in the '80 Olympics. Today, it wouldn't work. Tomorrow may be another question.

The collapse of the Soviet Union also marked the end of the famous Soviet system. Ten years ago the Fedorovs, Mogilnys, and Bures would have been trapped behind the Iron Curtain for life. Now for the first time they can finally show how Russians in their prime would compare to the best in the world every day of the week rather than just a few days a year.

Hockey fans had always dreamt of a truly global hockey league. Now it's finally arrived. The next decade could be the greatest in NHL history. The players profiled in the following pages are the brightest stars on the horizon—superstars who'll add glitter to hockey's golden decade. ★

Rod Brind'amour

He comes to play every night.

It's one of the oldest and silliest cliches in the coach's handbook. Yet it's still the greatest compliment a coach can pay to a player. It's true. Some players do come to watch on some nights. They're floaters. Players who coast by on talent without even breaking a sweat. They drive coaches crazy with their erratic work habits. Coaches usually come from the bluecollar working class. They tolerate talent and adore the workers, the muckers and grinders. When one of the lunch bucket brigade has a little talent to go along with his addiction to hard work, coaches fall head over heels in love.

St. Louis coach Brian Sutter thought he was looking in the mirror when he watched Rod Brind'amour play. Here was a kid who was the second coming of the most talented Sutter. In Brian Sutter's own words, "Rod Brind'amour is a big, strong kid who comes to play every night. He's a coach's dream." Sutter had that dream come to play for him every night for two years. He loved him almost like a brother.

BRIND'AMOUR

As a matter of fact, the only one he loved more was his own brother. Before the 1991–'92 season began he reluctantly approved a trade with Philadelphia. The Blues sent the 22-year-old Brind'amour and one of the league's most notorious floaters, Dan Quinn, to Philadelphia for Sutter's brother Ron, plus Murray Baron. The deal achieved two objectives. It got rid of the high-paid and low-producing Quinn and it completed a long-standing Sutter family project—uniting the twins, Ron and Rich. Brian Sutter knew the deal could come back to haunt the Blues.

Rod Brind'amour simply packed up his bags and his barbells and headed for one more stop on a journey that never seemed to end. Born in Ottawa, Ontario the road to Philadelphia had taken him through Prince Rupert and Campbell River, British Columbia; Wilcox, Saskatchewan; East Lansing, Michigan; and St. Louis. It was a journey that proved that destiny does not always take a direct route.

Brind'amour's father, Hubert ("Everybody calls me Bob"), was a pipefitter who moved from Ottawa to Prince Rupert when Rod was two. Bob was a self-confessed hockey nut who lived for Saturday night hockey on TV, plus any ice-time, day or night, that he could get in the rink. He worked the night shift so during the day he'd go to the empty rink to skate and shoot. He took two-year-old Roddy with him, put a helmet on his head, double-bladed skates on his feet, and gave him a chair to lean on and push around. Within a few months the chair had been replaced by a stick and the double-runners by a single blade.

Hockey was in his blood for life, but he may have been the youngest player to ever retire from the game. He quit twice, once when he was six and again when he was seven. His dad was heartbroken but he didn't push him to return to playing. He simply made sure he kept watching Hockey Night in Canada every Saturday night and by Christmas the seven year old had the bug again. This time for good. He told his dad he wanted to play hockey again and he never looked back.

His father, a native Quebecer, loved the Montreal Canadiens. His love-affair rubbed off on Rod. The flamboyant Guy Lafleur was his hero. A poster of Lafleur on his bedroom door was the last thing

BRIND'AMOUR

he looked at each night before he turned out the lights. He dreamed of becoming another Lafleur but when you live in rainy Prince Rupert those dreams are a far-fetched fantasy.

They seemed even more remote when the family moved to Campbell River on Vancouver Island. The climate was too warm to have outdoor ice and the town didn't even have an indoor rink until a year or two before the Brind'amours moved to town. Minor league hockey had just begun and Brind'amour quickly became a star. Hockey gave him an instant set of new friends in his new town. By now the game had become almost an obsession for Brind'amour but his parents made sure he retained perspective by getting Rod and younger brother Michel to play all sports. A natural all-round athlete, Brind'amour was also a star at softball and basketball.

But there was a time when he struggled in hockey, and for a very strange reason. The family wasn't wealthy and when his dad saw a pair of skates on sale he bought them for Rod, even though they were a size too large. He assumed he'd grow into them, but Rod never did. For a whole year the size nine-and-a-half floated around in ten-and-a-halfs. Yet he never complained or used them as an excuse.

With his father coaching and Rod playing defense, the kids from the little town of Campbell River shocked the kids from the big city and won the B.C. Triple A Bantam Championship. Even in skates that were too big, Brind'amour was a step above everyone else. The strongest part of his body was his mind. He played with his head, not his feet. His father the coach was amazed how Rod was always a step ahead of the rest of the team, anticipating the play. "He was smaller than the rest," his father recalls. "He was so smart with the puck and so much older than his years. He was always quiet, never affected by his success. He'd read stories written about him but never talk about them."

His father wasn't the only one who felt he had a future in hockey. The New Westminster Bruins had drafted him when he was twelve and when he wouldn't play for them they kept trading his rights around the league. His parents were determined to keep him out of major junior hockey. They wanted him to get an education. They gave him a choice between staying in his hometown or going to Notre Dame, **BRIND'AMOUR** that hockey factory in Wilcox, Saskatchewan. They'd never been there but they'd heard a lot about the school thanks to Russ Courtnall and Wendel Clark's success in the NHL.

It was an easy decision for the kid with NHL dreams. He chose Notre Dame. But it wasn't so easy on his parents. His father recalls the drive to the school: "It was so desolate, just a couple of trees and a few grain elevators. After leaving him there I felt so guilty I stopped the car and cried." Rod also thought he'd made a mistake. He was homesick. Every Sunday he'd phone home and there'd be long periods of silence. It was obvious he wanted to come home but he stayed until Christmas. Then a trip back home to Campbell River permanently cured his homesickness, as he wasn't able to make it back for Christmas for another seven years.

Rod grew at the school, packing on the pounds with a weightlifting program that would become a permanent part of his weekly routine for the rest of his life. The Hounds gave him a pair of skates that were the proper size. More importantly, they moved him to centre, his natural position. He became a star leading Notre Dame first to the Saskatchewan Triple A Midget Championships, and then to the Saskatchewan Junior title the next year. "It was a combination of things," says Brind'amour. "They concentrate on only two things, school and hockey. You don't have too many distractions other than that."

St. Louis agreed with his dad that he did have a future in hockey. They drafted him in the first round in 1988. He was the 9th player taken, right behind another unknown high school kid, Jeremy Roenick. The quietly maturing youngster from Campbell River didn't fall for the big money and glamour of the NHL. He knew he wasn't ready. He also knew there was life after hockey and he wanted to start preparing for it. He enrolled at the college hockey powerhouse, Michigan State.

It was the right move at the right time. "You

play against better players and you just naturally get better," says Brind'amour. "You get stronger and faster and learn more about the game. He learned a lot in his one year at Michigan State. The centre scored 59 points in 42 games and was named Freshman of the Year. It would be his last year of university hockey but not his last year of university. He still returns to Michigan State each summer to finish off his degree in business administration and marketing. A proud father says, "He's always been level-headed and determined. He knows hockey won't last forever."

After his freshman success, St. Louis called Brind'amour up for the playoffs. "It was the most nervous time of my life," he recalls. "But I actually got a goal in my first game on my first shot in the NHL. It was kind of neat. It helped me fit in quickly. It was a great time, but we didn't do well. We lost to Chicago, but it still was a great experience."

Chicago won in five games, but Brind'amour beat the butterflies in his stomach to score twice. The Blues pencilled him into their plans for 1989-'90. They planned on moving him to left wing to provide a defensive cover for the high-scoring combination of Brett Hull and Adam Oates.

Another Blue who'd made a career out of outworking everyone, the well-travelled Harold Snepts, remembers the rookie fondly. "I've never seen a guy work so hard in the last seven or eight years. He comes to the rink in his game face and he means business whether it's a game or practice."

The praise was mutual. Brind'amour was grateful for the support of the veterans. "Snepts and Paul MacLean helped me a lot. It was great." Despite the shift to an uncomfortable position that limited his range and talent, Brind'amour scored 26 goals and wound up with 61 points. Again in the playoffs, when the going got rough, Brind'amour got better. He had 13 points in 12 games and became only the second Blue ever named to the NHL's All-Rookie team.

His second year should have been better, but it wasn't. The Blues tried to ease the sophomore slump by moving him back to centre. He still slipped to 17 goals and 49 assists. Coach Brian Sutter felt Rod was putting too much pressure on himself but, as a lifetime overachiever, Sutter understood. "He puts a lot of expectations on himself, which is great," said Sutter. "If you don't expect a lot, you don't get a lot. We expect a lot from Roddy."

Brind'amour was in Chicago for a pre-season game in September, 1991 when he got the surprising news. The team that had drafted him, the team that loved his hard work had given up on him. They'd traded him to Philadelphia along with Dan Quinn for Ron Sutter and promising young defenseman Murray Baron. It was the saddest call home he'd made since his first year at Notre Dame. He was devastated, but his father reassured him it was the best thing that could have happened to him. St. Louis had turned him into a disciplined, defensive forward. In Philadelphia he'd have a chance to put the fun and the offense back into his game. They put him back at centre and he took off, getting a goal and an assist in his first game.

Brind'amour couldn't believe the difference in the two organizations. The new general manger, Russ Farwell, came out of the Western Hockey League and he brought with him an appreciation for kids from the west. He fired the driven and hard-driving coach Paul Holmgren and hired the likeable, fatherly Bill Dineen as coach. He brought in the mastermind of the WHL's Kamloops Blazers' success, Ken Hitchcock, as an assistant coach. For the first time in his NHL career Brind'amour felt he could relax. "Philadelphia is first class," he says. "Players are treated like real people."

At centre he had more skating room and had a chance to play the kind of hockey his father had taught him, disciplined yet inventive. No one had to worry about him relaxing too much. He was always hard working; even as a child his parents didn't have to call him twice in the morning. He'd be up at 5 a.m. waiting for his dad, packed and ready to go to the rink. Relaxed and having fun in Philly, Brind'amour had the year of his life, leading the Flyers in scoring all season long.

Rod Brind'amour has his own 52-member fan club spread across Canada. His father and mother in Campbell River; his younger brother Michel following in his skate steps at Notre Dame in Saskatchewan; and lots of aunts and uncles in Buckingham, Quebec, twenty miles from Ottawa. They remember young Roddie's prediction when he was just a toddler skating on double blades. As his father recalls, "He told us he was going to be rich some day, and he's right on track." ★

Pavel Bure

It was one of those bone-chilling early-winter nights in Vancouver when the rain seems to do the impossible—come up as well as down. Even with an umbrella it was futile to try to stay dry in an unrelenting downpour that seemed to penetrate everything. But there was something more than rain in the air on that November night—there was an aura of rare excitement and eager anticipation.

Only three days before this game, against a colorless team of Winnipeg Jets, there had been four thousand unsold seats. Now it was completely sold out. Scalpers stood in the pouring rain, in no hurry to sell off tickets for anything less than double or triple their face value. Vancouver hadn't seen anything like this since the opening night of the heavily-promoted Phantom of the Opera. Tonight, everyone wanted to be there for the opening of another phenomenon—the debut of the Phantom of the Coliseum—Pavel Bure. The twenty-year-old legend had reached near-mythic proportions in the two years since the Canucks had taken a wild gamble and chosen him in the sixth round of the 1989 draft. He was the 113th player chosen. Number 113 turned out to be Vancouver's lucky number.

BURE

The Canucks managed to steal him **BURE** supporting their claim and hinted at costly because of a technicality noted by their legal action if Ziegler ruled against them. sharp-eyed head of scouting, Mike Penny. An 18 When Bure arrived in North America two years year old couldn't be drafted after the third round later, the Canucks eagerly signed Bure to a contract unless he had played more than ten games in two only a few days before he would have become a free seasons in a major league. The NHL Media Guide agent. Even though he cost them nearly three mil- reported that Bure had played only five games the lion dollars the Canucks felt they had the bargain year before. But Penny did what no other NHL of the year.

official did; he looked beyond the Media Guide Pavel Bure wasn't always the best or fastest thing and discovered scoresheets that proved Bure had on ice. As a matter of fact the first time he stepped played eleven games that year. Other teams on the ice he had only one speed: stop. His father protested and then NHL President John Ziegler Vladimir, like so many other hopeful Dads, gave his threatened to declare Bure a free agent. He didn't six-year-old son a chair to push around to help his back down until the Canucks presented evidence balance. Pavel shakes his head and snickers as he

remembers, "I no move. I don't skate. I just stand there." It was the last time he stood still on the ice. He caught on. Very quickly. The way he's done everything in his life. His father recalls his son's first hockey tryout was a near washout. Pavel wore figure skates and stumbled and fell around the ice surface at the Red Army Sports School in Moscow. He was easily the worst player on the ice. Vladimir was not disappointed. After all, he wanted his son to be a swim- mer, just like Dad.

Vladimir Bure was a world-cham- pion swimmer, a product of a Soviet system that produced champions with assembly-line efficiency. Vladimir was good enough to stay on the high- ly competitive Soviet swim team for a dozen years. He swam in the Olympics in Mexico City in 1968 winning a bronze in the 4-by-200 relay. He was back in Munich in 1972, winning another bronze in the 200 relay and a silver in the 4-by-100 relay. He also finished third in anoth- er of Mark Spitz's historic seven gold- medal races, winning the bronze in the 50 metre freestyle. Vladimir Bure finished his career at the Montreal Olympics in 1976, fading to fourth in the 4-by-100 relay, and placing sev- enth in both the 50- and 200-metre freestyle.

Pavel was born in 1971, a year before **BURE** on speed, raising their games to a new level. Vladimir's career peaked in Munich. Naturally he hoped his son would follow in his wake. He started him swimming in the bathtub when Pavel was still an infant. As he grew older Pavel, nicknamed Pascha by the family, quickly grew bored with the repetitive monotony of doing laps, the necessary evil of training to become a world-class swimmer. He preferred the speed and variety of hockey. His father gave him two months to improve or get out of the rink forever. He warned him if he wasn't one of the best his hockey career would be over almost before it began. Even at six Pavel was highly competitive, very mature and extremely devoted—characteristics he'd inherited from his father.

Pavel was the newest branch of a very strong family tree. His ancestors were famous Swiss watchmakers. His great grandfather settled in Russia, bringing with him a Germanic determination and a Swiss love for precision and timing. All traits that helped mold Pavel's hockey career. He had the discipline to go to bed early each night so he'd be well-rested for a full day of hockey. No one ever had to persuade him to practise. He loved it. By the end of his first year he'd gone from being the worst player on the ice to being the best. It was a level he'd maintain throughout his childhood. He became so good and so fast that in some pick-up games the other kids made him play in boots, a handicap that turned out to be a benefit. It taught him the clever little moves that would someday drive NHL defensemen to distraction. Those pick-up games were among the happiest times of his childhood. He had an added incentive to play well and hard: if you lost you sat out the next game, a chilling thought in the sub-Arctic climate of his native Moscow.

His powerful skating and incredible flair for the game quickly caught the eye of the Soviet hockey system. His father had long ago given up his dreams of a swimming career for Pascha. Vladimir realized he had a hockey prodigy in the family. By the time he was 16, Pavel had moved on to the Central Red Army team. Coach Viktor Tikhonov was already developing plans for his star line of the '90s—Bure, Alexander Mogilny and Sergei Fedorov. Sergei, a couple of years older, became Pavel's best friend. They pushed each other in practise, speed feeding

on speed, raising their games to a new level. They both idolized the same boyhood hero, the original Russian Rocket, Valery Kharlamov. Watch films of Kharlamov driving the Canadians crazy in the super series of 1972 and you'll see a startling resemblance to Bure and Fedorov. Their explosive speed is frightening; just ask any NHL defenseman. Bure watched his hero in person and on TV and says humbly, "I will never be able to play as well as Kharlamov."

Bure was in Finland in 1989 with the Soviet National team when he learned the Vancouver Canucks had drafted him. He was flattered but in no rush to join the Russian exodus to the NHL. His goals remained patriotic—the NHL was a distant, vague entity to a boy raised on Soviet hockey. A boy in Moscow grows up dreaming of becoming another Kharlamov or Larionov, not another Howe or Hull. Bure was determined to win three gold medals at the World Championships before he even thought about joining the NHL.

After winning the gold in the 1990 World Championships, Bure was indicating he wouldn't be in Vancouver until the fall of 1992 at the earliest. Watching Bure score four goals in the Soviets five-game route to the gold at the Goodwill Games in Seattle, Pat Quinn was more convinced than ever that Bure could become a superstar in the NHL. He returned from Seattle talking about Bure's tremendous speed but even more impressed by his fearlessness in driving toward the net. "The Russians use his explosiveness to spread the defense," Quinn reported. "He was dangerous every shift down there."

Unfortunately for the Canucks, he still didn't seem in any rush to get to the NHL. He had a new goal. His 16-year-old brother Valeri was a rookie with the Red Army team, following his brother's climb up the Soviet hockey ladder. Pavel proudly boasted that Valeri was even better than he was at that age, and he wanted to stay and play on the same team together. A disheartened Pat Quinn admitted, "Bure won't be coming soon. 1992? 1994? Who knows?" Even in his wildest dreams Quinn couldn't have imagined that the answer would be 1991.

But the Bures, however, were no different than any other modern Russian family. Disillusioned by the collapse of the Soviet Union they worried about the future of their family and their **BURE** were incredible. One writer said, "If Winnipeg players are the Jets then what do you call Pavel Bure? How about the Rocket?" The Canucks most persistent media critic, Tony Gallagher, was moved to uncharacteristically glowing phrases. "Hip, hip, Bure," he wrote. "What else could you say after the first NHL game for Pavel Bure?"

country. With the defection of Alexander Mogilny and the loss of Sergei Fedorov there was increasing pressure on Bure to make a long-term commitment to the Red Army team. When he refused to sign on for another three years they punished him by not allowing him to join the Commonwealth of Independent States team at the Canada Cup. It was supposed to teach Bure a lesson. It did, but not the one Coach Tikhonov had hoped. Bure learned that his future in his homeland was as uncertain as the future of his homeland.

Early in the fall of 1991, the Bure family suddenly showed up at the Los Angeles airport. The internal politics of Soviet sport had become too intense. Family friend Serge Levin had put Vladimir in touch with player agent Ron Salcer who was based in Los Angeles. He arranged everything and welcomed the Bure family, father and two sons—mother stayed in Moscow—, into his Los Angeles home for several weeks while the politics intensified even further. The Soviets threatened to sue. The Canucks, already burned by a costly million-dollar mistake over Vladimir Krutov, were gun-shy about getting involved in another long legal battle. They let Salcer work things out with the Soviets before finally getting involved in negotiations with Bure. With the clock ticking toward an NHL-imposed deadline, the Canucks finally worked out a deal. Bure agreed to a four-year contract worth 2.7 million dollars. The problem was that Bure had no idea what a dollar was worth—all he wanted to do was play hockey again.

It didn't take Bure long to start repaying the Canucks investment. Vancouver was already being swept away by Canuck fever with Vancouver enjoying the greatest year in franchise history. They'd been in first place since opening day and would stay there until closing day. They were also enjoying one of their best seasons at the gate but it would get even better when Bure arrived. Pavelmania broke out immediately. A rumour that he'd play against the Jets less than a week after signing a contract started a run at the box office—4,000 unsold tickets were quickly snapped up.

The fans, even those who paid the scalpers' exhorbitant prices, got their money's worth. It was a debut to remember. The opening night reviews

In person, Bure looked even smaller and slighter than his listed 5' 9" and 165 pounds. But his size was irrelevant. After a summer off, the trainers testing the 20 year old were astounded. Perhaps it was in his genes, or perhaps it was from a lifetime of Soviet training techniques. Dr. Ted Rhodes of the University of British Columbia reported that Bure had less than six percent body fat. His anaerobic capacity seemed unlimited. He was also one of the strongest Canucks despite his small size, second only to physical fitness nut Doug Lidster in strength testing. Bure could bench press 200 pounds a dozen times without strain.

His strength created an explosive power that seemed to make him fly on the ice. A couple of short strides and he was in high gear. He stepped around Winnipeg defensemen like they were standing still on that opening night. The sellout crowd gasped in disbelief at some of his moves. Sixteen thousand fans would turn to each other in awe with a look that said, "Do you believe what he just did?" What he did that night was what he'd do for his first dozen NHL games. Dazzle the crowd and create terror in the defense with incredible end-to-end rushes that took your breath away but rarely produced anything except goosebumps. He led the league in near-goals.

Pat Quinn preached patience. He knew the promise would soon turn to production. He started Bure slowly, playing him on a line with the plodding Gino Odjick who would soon become his best friend and roommate. The third member of the Canucks fourth line was the veteran Ryan Walter. In his fourth game, Bure scored twice in Los Angeles, inspired by his first meeting with another of his boyhood idols, Wayne Gretzky. Gradually Quinn moved him up to a line with the more-talented Greg Adams and the Russian veteran Igor Larionov whose own game had risen to new heights since Bure's arrival. They became the Canucks' best line in the second half of the season, leading

the team to the second division title in club history and its first season above .500 in fifteen years.

BURE

The Russian Rocket carried the Canucks to new heights. Igor Larionov, who'd spanned the Soviet era between Kharlamov and Bure, compared his new teammate to a young Sergei Makarov with his explosive speed and inventive stickhandling. The Rocket blazed through the year improving with every game. He scored 26 goals in his last 27 games.

After watching Bure set up one goal and score another with a beautiful deflection to beat his New Jersey Devils 2–1, Coach Tom McVie said, "This kid is frightening. I'm glad he plays in the Smythe division and we only play them three times a year. I thought Fedorov was fast but this kid's even quicker. He's one of the best young players I've seen in a long, long time."

After missing the first 15 games of the year, Bure still finished with 34 goals, one less than the top-scoring rookie, Tony Amonte of the New York Rangers. Amonte mostly finished off exceptional plays by his linemate Mark Messier. Bure had to do most of the work himself. His goals were individual flashes of brilliance—a string of highlight clips that left mere mortals shaking their heads. One of his favourite moves came straight from road hockey. He'd drop the puck back into his feet, kick it up to his stick and then zip around embarrassed defensemen. Flashy, electrifying goals. But the one that astounded even the impossible to please—the old veterans, scouts and other curmudgeons of the rink—was the deflection he scored against McVie's Devils.

It was an unbelieveably simple move that proved Bure was a player with rare instinct and gift for the game. Canuck defenseman Jyrke Lumme fired a slapshot from the blueline. Bure, floating across the top of the face-off circle, casually twisted his wrists a fraction of an inch, the blade of his stick opening just enough to deflect the puck high into the top corner of the net, behind a goalie who never even moved. A goal so shocking in its simplicity that the crowd was stunned into silence for a second before roaring with disbelief. A goal that proved the Canucks finally had the franchise player who was worth waiting 22 years for.

In the playoffs in his rookie season Bure won the

ultimate compliment—the wrath of Hockey Night in Canada's resident redneck, Don Cherry. He had his own nickname for the Russian Rocket, calling him a little weasel, and accusing him of being sneaky and disappearing into a hole when the going got tough. Fans in Vancouver took the insult personally and made Cherry's life miserable in Vancouver. Bure shrugged it off, "What is weasel? I no know," he said. "Who is this Cherry?"

Bure worried more about the compliment the Winnipeg Jets were paying him than the insult fired at him by the bombastic Mr. Cherry. The Jets felt if they could shut down Bure they could shut down the Canucks. They came at him with sticks and elbows high everytime he came near the puck. Pat Quinn understood it was part of the NHL's ancient hazing ritual for rookies. "In open ice Pavel can make great plays," says Quinn. "He's got to learn to compete. He's black and blue from the waist up from all the shots he's taking. The referees don't give him a break. But he's getting a lot smarter. He's stopped retaliating."

Frustrated by the tight and often illegal checking, Bure did struggle early in the opening round of the playoffs. The Canucks fell behind three games to one and were within a loss of having their finest season end in embarrassment. Faced with elimination, Bure came through with his finest game in a Canuck uniform. He scored one goal and set up three others as Vancouver humiliated the Jets 8 to 2. Deflated Winnipeg never recovered. In game six, Bure's hat-trick did the impossible, shutting up both the rabid fans in Winnipeg and Don Cherry. The Canucks finished off the comeback with a 5–0 win in Vancouver. Bure ended the series with 5 goals and 8 points, seven of them in those two key games.

The comeback took a lot out of the Canucks. The well-rested Edmonton Oilers continued the assault on Bure that the Jets had started. The NHL's most annoying and maybe best checker Esa Tikkanen teamed-up with the veteran defenseman Kevin Lowe to shut down Bure almost completely. He was held to one goal and one assist as Vancouver's dream season ended in a four games to two loss to the Oilers.

The Stanley Cup would have to wait for another year, but Bure did accomplish what no Canuck had ever done before—win the prestigious Calder

Trophy for NHL Rookie of the Year. Said his coach Pat Quinn, "Bure's going to be a superstar in the league for a long time to come."

Bure looked back on the most chaotic six months in his life with satisfaction and enjoyment.

BURE

"I never hear fans like this," he says. "In Moscow fans are very quiet. Here, they're crazy. I love it. It's fun for me, playing in the NHL. Next year I have more fun and the fans have more fun too." The fans can't wait.   ★

Gilbert Dionne

What's in a name? Obviously there's a natural scoring ability if that name is Dionne.

What's in a name? Pride when your name is Dionne and your older brother is one of the greatest scorers in NHL history.

What's in a name? Great expectations and increased pressure when you're the younger brother of a hockey legend.

"I went through a lot," admits Gilbert Dionne, who's been trying to skate out from under his brother's shadow all of his young life. "I'm very proud to be his brother, it's just that sometimes I wish he wouldn't be in my career. You know what I mean?"

DIONNE

What he means is that everything Gilbert Dionne does on and off the ice is instantly measured against the incredible accomplishments of Marcel Dionne. Gilbert chuckles that, "Maybe I should go and have a blood test and find out if he's really my brother or my father or whatever. With the age difference it's hard to tell."

Marcel is old enough to be Gilbert's father. Marcel was 19 years old and already on his way to becoming the NHL's third-highest leading scorer when Gilbert was born. Marcel was a rookie with Detroit—a Quebec native trying to prove his beloved Montreal Canadiens had made a mistake by passing him up to make Guy Lafleur their first choice in the 1971 draft. It would take him eighteen years to do it. Marcel Dionne retired in third position on the all-time scoring list with 1,771 points, 420 more than Lafleur who retired in eighth position. Marcel played in Detroit and Los Angeles—it would be twenty years after Marcel started before a Dionne finally played in a Montreal uniform.

Growing up thousands of miles apart, the Dionne brothers spent little time together and had little except hockey in common. Gilbert reveals, "Marcel helped me out off the ice with money and the usual brotherly stuff, but I really didn't see him that much when I was growing up."

One big difference between the two brothers is that Gilbert grew up a lot more than Marcel did. Marcel was a compact (an NHL euphemism for undersized) 5' 8", 185 pounds. If he'd been Gilbert's size, 6' 0", 195 pounds, he and not Lafleur would have been Montreal's first choice in 1971. The size made the two brothers different in skills and position. Marcel was a shifty centre. He had to be to avoid the pounding that would have shortened his career. Gilbert developed into a grinder, a winger who has to work his way out of the corners and into scoring position by strength as much as skill.

The brothers did have one thing in common. They were among the few Quebec kids who preferred to play in Ontario. Marcel was a junior superstar with the St. Catherine's Blackhawks of the Ontario Hockey League. When he returned home in the summer of 1987 he realized his kid brother might have a future in hockey. But not in Quebec. He could see that Gilbert was a plugger

DIONNE

who might get lost in the wide-open Quebec League. NHL scouts have grown wary of Quebec junior stars who put incredible scoring numbers on the board. They rarely even bother looking at less-flashy grinders like Gilbert. He convinced Gilbert to go to the Ontario League where his scoring statistics might be smaller but where his chances of being drafted were greater. He could also work on his defense.

Marcel's advice and his reputation paid off. The Kitchener Rangers never saw him play but because he was a Dionne they took a chance on him in the 19th round of the 1987 draft of graduates from midget hockey. They sent him to their Niagara Falls Junior B club where the untested kid from Quebec proved he could play in Ontario. He scored 36 goals in 38 games and won a job in Kitchener for the next two years.

His rookie season in Kitchener was a struggle. He had a difficult time winning a regular spot on a team that included several future NHL first round draft choices including world junior star Stephen

Rice. Dionne got just 11 goals in his first year in the OHL, but he was starting to feel at home in Kitchener.

In his second year, his play blossomed into the solid, quietly productive style that would be an omen of equally surprising things to come in the NHL. With 48 goals and 105 points he helped Kitchener make a run at the Ontario Hockey League championship. He was even better in the playoffs, scoring 13 goals and 23 points in a 17-game run that came within only a lucky bounce of a trip to the Memorial Cup. Kitchener lost a heartbreaking double-overtime thriller to Eric Lindros and the Oshawa Generals.

The Rangers had lost, but Dionne came out a winner. "I didn't really expect to be drafted very high and I certainly never expected to go to Montreal," he said, well aware that he still had a lot of work to do on his defense and his quickness. But Montreal liked what it saw of Dionne in the playoffs. They also may have still felt guilty about passing up his brother twenty years earlier. They took him in the fifth round as a long-range project, a young player who would need a lot of time in the minors and might never make it to the NHL.

Dionne was happy to go to Fredericton in the American Hockey League. He was still trying to get over the shock of being drafted by the Canadiens: "I knew Pat Burns really stressed defense and that wasn't my strength." Burns also stressed patience with young players: "We knew he could score and we were willing to wait for him to develop the rest of his game."

It didn't take long. A little over a year in Fredericton would do it. Dionne had no trouble adjusting to the faster pace and heavier hitting of the American League. He produced 40 goals and 87 points in 77 games. It still wasn't enough to win a permanent promotion to the Canadiens after the 1991–'92 training camp. He'd just celebrated his 21st birthday and he had time and patience on his side. He went back to New Brunswick for 29 games and started to score like Marcel Dionne—19 goals and

DIONNE

46 points won him a trip back to Montreal, to stay.

The once explosive Montreal Canadiens had done the unthinkable; they'd turned into a boring, plodding team that scored as seldom as it entertained. They needed a spark-plug. A French Canadian spark-plug preferably. They got both. Dionne's scoring put new life in an old body—Denis Savard's. He moved to Savard's left wing and the rest became Montreal scoring history. Dionne scored 20 goals in his first 34 games; 21 goals and 34 points in less than half a season in Montreal. "My teammates helped me a lot," he said modestly. "Especially Denis. I just hang around. He does all the work and I just finish it. He gets lots of assists and I get lots of goals."

His goals weren't spectacular, dashing and daring like the Flying Frenchmen of the past, Cournoyer and Lafleur. They were more workmanlike efforts, the kind that Marcel had made a family tradition. "He goes to the net and stays there," notes Savard. "You know that's where all the goals are scored. A lot of goals are going to be produced in a radius of ten feet around the net and that's where he stays. He's really good at it. He gets position and he uses his stick very well."

Savard was convinced Dionne was no scoring flash in the pan. Pat Burns biggest concern was that Dionne would be a victim of "Le Burnout." The French-speaking fans and media put so much pressure on young French stars that they eventually buckle and burn out. Stephane Richer and Claude Lemieux were recent victims. And the fans expect even more from a kid with a name like Dionne.

Comparisons with his brother are still inevitable and tiresome, but Gilbert feels the worst is behind him. The best still lies ahead. "I'm 21 years old and I'm happy I can deal with it (the comparisons and the pressure). I can speak for myself. I've proven I can play in this league and I'm just happy to be a part of the Montreal Canadiens organization."

Ahh, to be young and a Dionne in Montreal! ★

Pat Falloon

The San Jose Sharks turned out to be the expansion team that never was: it never was really treated like an expansion team. Yes, it got to pick the castoffs and unwanted players from the rest of the league, the traditional way to stock an expansion franchise. But it didn't get to pick the best of the junior players in the world, a right normally reserved for new teams in the league.

San Jose had followed a strange route to the NHL. The Gund brothers, George and Gordon, were absentee owners of the Minnesota North Stars. They'd originally entered the league in 1977 when they bought the Cleveland Barons. When the Cleveland franchise floundered they merged it with another struggling team in Minnesota. After 15 years of trying to run businesses on the west coast and a hockey team in the midwest they agreed to sell the North Stars as long as the NHL gave them a new team closer to home. The league agreed to let them establish a team in San Jose and enter the NHL a year ahead of expansion teams in Ottawa and Tampa Bay.

FALLOON

Fearing a revolt in Quebec, the NHL wouldn't let San Jose have the **FALLOON** first pick in the junior draft which, as an expansion team, they would normally expect. Any other year there might not have been any complaints, but with Eric Lindros coming of age the Quebec Nordiques didn't want a new team stealing their first pick away. But the Sharks didn't complain too loudly. They were perfectly happy with having second choice. They got to take a player who may never make the headlines or have the impact of a Lindros, but would still be a vital building block for a new team.

"Pat Falloon was everything we expected him to be and more," said San Jose General Manager Jack Ferreira after Falloon's rookie year. "He progressed the way we thought he would. He proved at training camp that he could play in this league. He had his problems when the pace picked up during the season but then he got used to it and showed us what he could do."

What he could do was skate and shoot as well as any NHLer and pass better than most. They were skills he grew on the farm, back home in Foxwarren, Manitoba. It's a sleepy farming town about 200 miles northwest of Winnipeg. "There probably aren't more than a hundred people left in the town," he says. "But we were lucky enough to have our own rink. Like most prairie kids my favourite TV show was Hockey Night in Canada. All I ever wanted to do was play hockey."

The Falloon farm was about five miles out of town but he never had any trouble getting to the rink. Despite its small size, Foxwarren was the centre of a large farming area and had a very active minor league hockey program that drew kids and coaches from miles around. Pat Falloon started playing regularly when he was six years old and he rarely stopped. "I was definitely in the rink-rat category," he chuckles. "I was on the ice every chance I got. The rink was right across from school and we'd go over at noon and skate and shoot. We had lots of pretty good coaching but the game always seemed to be pretty easy for me. I played a little centre, but most of the time I was a right winger. My hero was Guy Lafleur. I'd try to play just like he did."

Falloon did a good enough Lafleur impersonation to start drawing attention as one of the best young right wingers in the province of Manitoba. When he was 15 he starred in the provincial Triple A Midget league with Yellowhead, a town about 25 miles from the farm. In just 52 games he scored 74 goals and 143 points. Despite his scoring success, the Regina Pats who'd drafted his junior rights had some concerns about his size, so they traded him to Spokane, Washington.

At only 15 years old the kid who'd never really been off the family farm packed his bags and moved south of the border. "Some guys have trouble with being homesick but my parents were really supportive and I never had any problems," he says gratefully. "It was an adjustment for sure moving away from home, but as it turned out it was the best move I ever made." Spokane was stockpiling young talent. No one was panicking when Falloon and his teammates weren't very good in that first year. "We could see we were on the right track," he says. "Everybody got along really well right off the bat. The only disappointment was missing the playoffs."

He'd formed a quick alliance with centre Ray Whitney, another talented playmaker. They were close both on and off the ice. Whitney helped Falloon score 60 goals and 124 points in his second year. This time they made the playoffs, only to lose in six games to a powerhouse team from Kamloops that would go on to lose the finals of the Memorial Cup. The Western league would have to wait another year to win the cup.

That championship team would come from Spokane. "Losing to Kamloops the year before made us more determined than ever," says Falloon. "We thought we had a pretty good team and then when we made a deal to get (goaltender) Trevor Kidd a couple of months before the playoffs, we knew we had a definite shot at it." That shot turned out to be a guided missile that carried them past every hurdle without a falter. They won 14 of 15 playoff games en route to the 1991 Memorial Cup.

It was the most incredible period of Falloon's young hockey career. "We really came together as a team. You knew before you went out you were going to win every night." And they did nearly every night with Falloon on a record scoring pace. He'd improved in every offensive category during the year, scoring 64 goals and 138 points to finish fourth in league scoring. During the playoffs he was even deadlier, scoring 10 goals and 24 points in 15 games. And in the Memorial Cup finals he scored an incredible 12 points in four games, including 8 goals to tie a Memorial Cup record held by a couple of pretty fair scorers named Dale Hawerchuk and Luc Robitaille.

"To have my name in the record book alongside those two guys is one of the biggest thrills of my life. That whole trip to Quebec for the Memorial Cup was incredible." The run to the cup had kept his mind off another big event in his life—the NHL draft. Everyone had known for years Eric Lindros would be taken number one. The modest Falloon was the last person expecting to be chosen number two. "I didn't have a clue where I'd be drafted," he said. "I bounced around on scouting lists all during my last year in Spokane. I'd been ranked anywhere from third to tenth. Most people expected Scott Neidermayer (a Kamloops defenceman) to be taken second. When San Jose chose me I couldn't believe it. I was overwhelmed. I figured it gave me a better chance to make the NHL."

The Sharks were as excited as Falloon. They felt he could be a star in the NHL someday. But they didn't want to put him under the public pressure of being called a "franchise player," the superstar every team needs to win a Stanley Cup.

Assistant coach Bob Murdoch explained, "Nobody expects him to lead us out of the wilderness by himself. We've gone out of our way to avoid building him up so big that the fall could kill him." Physically, Falloon graded high in every skill level. Skating: as quick as anyone inside the blueline. Passing: already one of the best passing wingers in the NHL. Shooting: a hard accurate shot with a quick release. The Sharks only complaint was a rare one for a young player. Coach George Kingston felt he didn't shoot enough.

FALLOON

"He's got one of the best shots in the league. He's got to start using it more. His biggest problem is that he's not selfish enough."

Falloon's heard that complaint before. "I probably dish off the puck more than I should," he says. "I don't know why but I've always done that. I look for the pass first and then I shoot as a last resort. I agree with the coach. I've got to work on that and my defense. I guess it's a problem every young player goes through. When you grow up you're used to playing on the line that does all the scoring. Other teams put checkers on you and they're never a real threat to score so you don't even think about playing defense."

He also didn't think much about losing until he went to San Jose. He went to training camp cautiously optimistic that he could make the team. "I'd always thought I could play in the NHL some day, but you're never really sure. Playing on the Canadian team that won the gold medal at the 1991 World Junior Championships had helped a lot. The pace there was quicker than in junior and it turned out to be about the same as in the NHL."

The Sharks never doubted Falloon's ability but they started to wonder if some doubters had been right about his size. He was listed anywhere from 5' 9" to 5' 11", and from 170 to 192 pounds. "Call me anything you want," Falloon laughs. "I'm somewhere in that range," he adds without revealing his true size. He'd been quick enough to survive in junior but in the NHL there were some questions. Especially when he was scratched from the opening night lineup with an injury. Fortunately, it turned out to be the only game he'd miss all season. Coach Kingston was delighted with the Shark's first bite in the draft. "Patty's 19 going on 29. He suffered through one bad month when he got down on himself a little. But he's an awfully mature young man. He pulled himself out of it. We couldn't have asked for more from any player."

Falloon scored his first NHL goal in the third game of his career, against Calgary. He scored again four nights later. But he wouldn't score again for nearly a month. He went through an eleven-game scoring drought. "It was the worst period of my life," he recalls. "Everybody in San Jose was great. The fans gave us tremendous support but it was hard to go out there and lose every night. We were getting blown out. We didn't win any of those eleven games. I'd never gone through anything like it before. I lost a lot of confidence."

He got it back with a little help from the coaches and a lot of help from his roommate, Brian Lawton. "He'd been the number one pick in the draft (in 1983), and he'd struggled. He'd gone through a lot of ups and downs. He showed me the ropes and I really thank him for that." Lawton got all the thanks he wanted watching the shy kid from the tiny town in the middle of nowhere develop into

FALLOON

the closest thing there is to a hockey star in the San Francisco Bay area. "I told him not to worry about carrying the weight of the entire franchise on his shoulders," says Lawton. "He can't do anymore than his own job. He's naive about a lot of things and I try to help him as much as I can. He's very level-headed and comes from a great family. He'll be okay."

Falloon came out of that early season slump to lead the Sharks in scoring. It all started to turn around in late November when he played his first game in Edmonton. His parents drove ten hours from their home in Manitoba to watch him score twice, including a dramatic goal with twelve seconds left in the third period to give San Jose a 4–4 tie with the Oilers. That was one of his fondest memories of his rookie season. "It was great to be able to make their long trip worthwhile."

It was just as much fun in January when half the town of Foxwarren travelled to Winnipeg to see the home-town boy make good in his first NHL game back in Manitoba. Again he came through for the friends and fans in the stands. This time he waited even longer to supply the dramatic conclusion of an exciting game. He scored the winner with eight seconds to play as San Jose upset the Jets 4–3. Coach Kingston wasn't surprised. "He's going to score a lot of goals like that in this league. He's quick and he's got great hands. But if you just look at the points you don't get the whole picture. If you put his first year into perspective you'll see that if he plays with a little more determination, especially on defense, he could be a real star."

High praise for a kid who insists he's "just a normal kind of guy." Normal enough to return home for the summer where his father Ron promised "to put him back to work on the tractor." He helped his dad and uncle work their 3,000 acres, but once a week he'd slip away to a summer hockey league in Brandon where he was treated "just like a normal kind of guy." He played a little hockey, had a little fun and followed the coach's orders. He started shooting more. It worked in the summer league. Now Pat Falloon can't wait to try it out in his winter job. ★

Sergei Fedorov

The NHL All-Star game has become an annual parody of the modern NHL. It's a wide-open, free-wheeling, last-shot-wins affair where defense is accidental, not intentional. It's a showcase for everyone but the goalies, the sitting ducks in the all-star rifle range. Twenty minutes after it's over no one remembers who won or lost, just as they can't recall who finished first in the regular season once the playoffs begin. But 20 years later hockey fans will remember many of the winners in the skills contest which began as a made-for-TV excuse to sell more tickets and commercials and now threatens to supplant the game as the best part of All-Star weekend in the NHL.

Before the 1991–'92 season began, a host of hockey magazines published features that rated the best in the league at various skills. The ratings were based entirely on reputation. The lists of fastest skaters were always headed by Paul Coffey, generally followed by Steve Yzerman, Paul Ranheim, Trevor Linden and Pat LaFontaine. Detroit's sensational sophomore Sergei Fedorov was ranked second best on breakaways and the fifth most exciting player in one poll.

FEDOROV

But, until All-Star weekend, no one ranked him among the top five speed-burners in the league. When it was over he still wasn't listed in the top five—he was in a category of his own, a mile ahead of every other skater in the league. Coffey, slowed by knee and back injuries that plagued the twilight of his career, wasn't even in the running. Linden was also among the also-rans, sidelined early in a simple race—one fast lap around the rink. When it was Fedorov's turn to skate the fans in Philadelphia were left almost breathless by his speed. He literally flew around the rink with an effortless ease, nearly a second faster than some of the quickest skaters in the league.

His only real competition came from his old Russian roommate, Alexander Mogilny. Together, they blew away the field. After it was over, TV commentator Bill Clements, a journeyman player who'd made an NHL career out of using extraordinarily hard work to compensate for ordinary talent, looked at Fedorov in awe and asked how he managed to skate so fast. Fedorov stared back at him in disbelief that he could ask such a naive question. Finally Fedorov replied matter of factly, "I make my feet go as fast as they can." The great ones always have trouble explaining their gift to the less talented. To them it is that simple. Make your feet go fast. Shoot as hard as you can. Put the puck where the goaltender isn't. That's all Sergei Fedorov has been trying to do since he learned the game on the frozen ponds and rinks of his hometown near the Russian port of Murmansk.

He was a natural. The game always came easily to this prodigy on skates. His father Viktor was doubly delighted by his son's precociousness. He was both proud parent and happy coach. Young Sergei, nicknamed Fedye by family and friends, was always the star of every team he played for. His father was the coach of every one. But in the Soviet Union all hockey roads lead to Moscow. The Soviet feeder system funnels the best prospects in the country into the Central Red Army club in Moscow.

At 15, Fedye found himself a thousand miles from home, rooming with another shy, quiet teenager from the Soviet outback—Alexander Mogilny. They would eventually follow another similar road to the NHL but at 15 they were the

FEDOROV

Chosen Ones. The hand-picked successors to the Fantastic Five, the famous first unit of the Red Army and Soviet National team: Vladimir Krutov, Igor Larionov, Sergei Makarov, Viacheslav Fetisov and Alexei Kasatonov.

Fedorov and Mogilny would soon be joined by the equally speedy Pavel Bure to form a line that would keep the Soviet vault full of gold medals through the turn of the century. This generation of Soviet hockey players was even better than the last. They were bigger and tougher. They proved that in that infamous Canada–USSR junior game in Czechoslovakia in 1987. It became the black eye of international hockey, ending in a brawl that didn't finish until they literally turned out the lights in the arena. When the lights went out the 6' 1", 195 pound Fedorov was still there, swinging with the best of them.

Recognizing the Canadian strategy of trying to intimidate the smaller, more skilled Soviets, the Red Army's four star hockey general, Viktor Tikhonov had taught Fedorov and his teammates to slap the other cheek, not turn it. When the going got tough the Soviets didn't get shaken anymore. Unwittingly, Tikhonov was also preparing the Soviets perfectly for a future in the rough, tough, high-sticking world of the NHL. In 1989 Fedorov moved up to the national team and helped them win another World Championship. The NHL was starting to take notice. The Detroit Red Wings decided to risk a fourth round draft choice on Fedorov. At that point it was the highest any Soviet had gone in the draft. He'd have been the first or second choice but the NHL expected him to play another ten years in the Soviet Union.

Detroit took a chance on the advice of their captain, Steve Yzerman. He'd played against Fedorov in the World Championships and was impressed by Sergei's speed. He was even more amazed by his feistiness. Fighting is not allowed at the World Championship but Fedorov was always willing to rub a glove in the face of anyone who got a little too chippy. "It was the way I was taught to play the game," he says matter of factly. "It was the way I've always played."

Back in the Soviet league Fedorov was finding it hard to stay interested in the mediocre hockey that's a fact of life in a very unbalanced league. He

scored only 19 goals in 48 games for a **FEDOROV** world. Detroit's new coach and general
Red Army team that continued its manager, Bryan Murray, didn't have to
monopoly of the Soviet championship. He was be told. He'd seen for himself. He coached Canada
growing weary of the 11 months of the year grind of in a loss to the Soviets and agreed with Yzerman.
hockey life for members of the Soviet national team. "Sergei was hard-working and talented," says Murray. "He's not afraid of traffic. He checks well, he's
His roommate Mogilny had defected a year earlier versatile, and best of all he doesn't shy away from
and urged Sergei to go with him. He'd refused but the tough stuff."
now he was starting to have second thoughts.
Detroit had softened him up the summer before at Murray was more determined than ever to get
the Soviet training camp in Helsinki, Finland. They Fedorov into the NHL as soon as possible. His
met briefly with Fedorov and another of their draft chance came that summer when Fedorov was part
choices, Vladimir Konstantinov. Fedorov politely of the Soviet squad at the Goodwill Games in
accepted the letter in Russian, explaining the Red Seattle. He'd already told the Soviets he wanted to
Wings had drafted him but he refused to offer join his old pal Mogilny and the increasing number
Detroit any hope. The Red Wings went away dis- of Soviets playing in the NHL. "There was no
couraged, interpreting his coolness as disinterest. future in the Soviet Union," he said sadly.
They didn't realize it was just part of his personality.
The way he reacted to almost everything. But the Soviets refused to give Fedorov his
release so he left on his own. He walked away after
The next spring Fedorov led the Soviets to an exhibition game in Portland, Oregon and didn't
another world title in Bern, Switzerland. Again resurface until a couple of days later at a news con-
Yzerman played against him and came away con- ference in Detroit. The Red Wings had signed the
vinced Fedorov was the best 20 year old in the "best 20 year old in the world" to a five-year contract. The $250,000 a year wasn't much by Gretzky
or Lemieux standards, but it was a fortune to the
young man who couldn't even get his own apart-
ment in Moscow.

Fedorov moved into a high rise, a slapshot away
from Detroit's Joe Louis Arena. He treated himself
to a new sports car, something he couldn't have
bought in the Soviet Union even if he'd had the
money. Best of all, he didn't have to cut off his
links to his homeland. Unlike Mogilny, Fedorov
wasn't technically a defector or a Red Army deserter. Naturally the Soviets complained and wanted
him back but when it was obvious he was staying
they dropped the protests and even allowed him to
play for them in the Canada Cup in 1991.

It didn't take the Red Wings long to know they
had the real thing on their hands. Any thought
that Fedorov might be intimidated by the thugs in
the NHL disappeared in the drop of the gloves at
his first training camp. His roommate Shawn Burr
warned him not to put up with any of the gooning
the NHL seems to feel is a rite of passage for Europeans. They've usually run the gauntlet of high
sticks and butt ends in their first spin around the
league. How they respond to that initial trial by
elbows will decide how they'll be treated for the
whole year and possibly their entire career. Fedorov
didn't give an inch; he rose to the challenge.

didn't give an inch; he rose to the challenge.

FEDOROV

The shy, quiet Russian was the first player to drop the gloves at his first workout with the Red Wings. He was high-sticked by Al Conroy, a tough little career minor leaguer trying desperately to catch the attention of management. Coach Murray was startled and secretly delighted to watch Fedorov risk his million-dollar hands slugging it out with the quickly-forgotten Conroy. A couple of days later Fedorov got high-sticked by another nobody. One week into his NHL career, Sergei Fedorov looked like he'd been in the league forever. He had one black eye and five stitches over the other. "No problem," he shrugged in his halting English. "Is the way the game is played."

The coach's only concern about Fedorov was how he'd handle the pressure. Everyone who watched his incredible flying feet and the quick flick that sent pucks rocketing into the net had predicted that Fedorov would become the NHL's first Soviet superstar. Murray tried to head off the burden of great expectations. "If he eventually gives us 25–35 goals a season, we'll be very happy."

Fedorov didn't do much to lessen the pressure. In his very first NHL game, number 91 scored his first goal, taking a pass from Yzerman and snapping the puck past Sean Burke in the New Jersey net. The 20-year-old couldn't understand what all the fuss was about. "I wasn't nervous, just very tired," he recalls. The rest of his rookie season came as easily and naturally as every other season of his life. He led all rookies in scoring with 31 goals, 48 assists, 79 points. He'd surpassed Murray's modest goals. The coach had discovered an added bonus— Fedorov was his best defensive forward. Opposing players like Chicago's Trent Yawney discovered the willowy-looking Fedorov was deceptively powerful. "He's a typical Russian," says Yawney. "Trying to move him is like trying to move a building."

The years of developing in the Red Army system paid unexpected dividends. He'd grown up playing with players years older and much stronger. He'd learned to compensate with speed and skill. Murray used him to centre the checking line. Playing against the superstars like Gretzky and Lemieux night after night, Fedorov still finished the year with a solid plus-minus rating of plus 11. Al Arbour, who'd coached a couple of superstars named Bossy and Trottier predicted he was going to become one of the league's great ones.

That summer he settled into life in Detroit, discovering the North American joys of baseball, golf and fishing. Baseball remained a mystery but golf became almost as big a passion for Fedorov as for his old pal Mogilny who was hooked on the game. He struggled to learn English and improved enough to help out in a summer hockey school where his actions spoke much louder and more clearly than his words. The kid came out in the 21-year-old at the end of each day when he became a 15-year-old again, romping around the ice, keeping the puck away from a yelping pack of youngsters in a good old-fashioned game of shinny.

The only disappointment of his first year was not winning the Calder trophy as top rookie. It went to Chicago's great goaltender, Ed Belfour. "I not disappointed," says Fedorov. "I did my best. I learned a lot. Next year will be easier." Reporters tried to get him to predict a 50 goal season. Anything seemed possible for the incredibly talented Fedorov, but he wisely refused to be trapped by foolish predictions. All he'd promise was that he'd do better. Even that proved to be difficult.

His sophomore season was not the next step to superstardom everyone had predicted. Even though he continued to amaze with his raw talent and blinding speed, his final numbers were almost identical to his rookie season. Like all Russians groomed by Tikhonov, he sublimated his individuality, worrying only about team success. His biggest fan remained Bryan Murray who is convinced Fedorov will become a superstar someday.

Fedorov isn't concerned. He's just happy that his future is not limited by the stifling greyness of life in his homeland. "It gives me warm feeling that the public accepts me here," he said. "I'm very glad they like my hockey." Sergei—they love it. ★

Theoren Fleury

If Japanese scientists were asked to mass produce hockey players they'd all come off the assembly line looking like Theoren Fleury. Short. Compact. Powerful. Like all those Japanese cars, he's indestructible and runs forever on a small tank of gas.

Picture Theoren Fleury and you don't see him scoring any of the 129 goals he scored in 275 NHL games. The pictures that emerge from the Fleury memory-bank are of the little guy leaping off his skates to flatten some unsuspecting giant who probably has kids at home bigger than Fleury. They both go down in a tangle of legs and arms. Fleury is always the first to pop back up on his skates, pushing his helmet back into place and cockily skating away with a swagger as if to say, "Who's the tough guy now?"

FLEURY

Small is a state of mind, not body. Fleury's spent his life looking up at people, looking not in fear but in anticipation, knowing he's going to get hit. Preparing for it and then, like a clever fighter, waiting for an opening to deliver the knockout punch. If you don't have size and muscle, you learn to compensate with intelligence and cunning. Fleury is the fox skating with a pack of wolves. "I learned early," he says. "Whenever I have the puck I have to be aware of who's on the ice: who's likely to hit me and who's likely to turn away."

Fleury had to learn early to survive. His father was 5' 8" tall; his mother barely reached five feet. It was obvious when he was born in Oxbow, Saskatchewan that he would never be a giant. He was so tiny at birth that his mom named him after the hero of one of her favorite movies, the Walt Disney classic, *Old Yeller*. Naturally the hero was the smallest person in the movie.

His father got a job driving heavy equipment for the town of Russell, Manitoba, about 90 miles northeast of his birthplace. Money was never a problem. There was never any extra so Fleury never expected any. He recalls that he never had a pair of skates that wasn't borrowed until he started playing junior hockey. If their team travelled to tournaments, Fleury had to rely on someone else to pay his way. That kind of generosity could weaken and wear out some children. They become embarrassed and drift away from the situations that put them in need. But it merely intensified Fleury's drive and resolve to never have to borrow again.

It may have been the birthplace of the chip on his shoulder. If he wasn't as good as everyone else away from the rink he'd certainly prove he was better than anyone else on the ice. He'd do anything to win. The stick and the sneak attack would become the great equalizer. He was described as a mosquito with an attitude problem. He was actually more like the Tasmanian Devil, that cartoon character that buzzsaws through life attacking everything in its path with gleeful abandon. On his arrival in Calgary years later he expressed his philosophy by simply and realistically telling reporters, "If a little guy like me is to succeed in the big leagues I have to show all those guys, big or small, that I'll stand up for my rights. I don't care if it's Jeff Beukeboom or Mario Lemieux that I hit."

FLEURY

It was a style developed in the battlefield of minor hockey on the prairies. He grew up in the kind of harsh climate jokingly described as ten months of winter and two months of slush. Fleury, the ultimate rink rat, perfected his style in the never-ending hockey games of his youth. By the age of 16 he was good enough to play for the Moose Jaw Warriors of the Western Hockey League. No one thought he had a chance to make it to the NHL. The way he played, no one thought he had a chance of even living long enough to reach the draft age of 18.

The Little Big Man was the only one who never doubted his ability to play with the bigger boys. His career had almost ended a couple of years earlier in bantam hockey. His right arm was badly cut by a skate blade. It sliced through his artery causing nerve damage that still leaves him without feeling in parts of his right hand. He missed nearly a full year of hockey. It only increased his already-intense drive and desire. Hockey wasn't the main thing in his life—it was the only thing!

Pickup hockey games had taught him a valuable lesson. If a little guy like him gave up the puck, he'd never get it back. He developed the stickhandling, the speed and the clever little spin moves that helped him dart and dive away from the big kids. It didn't take him long to raise his skills to the level he needed to dominate in junior hockey as well. By his second year he was team leader. By his third and fourth years in junior he was a superstar. During the 1987–'88 year, his last year of junior, he scored 68 goals and 160 points, tying for the scoring lead with Swift Current's Joe Sakic.

He'd heard the whispers of scouts, suggesting that despite his big numbers in the high-scoring WHL he'd never make it in the NHL. For the first time in his life he started to wonder if maybe they were right. Maybe his dream was unrealistic. Those doubts disappeared, however, when he was invited to the training camp for the National Junior team. The best juniors in the country were there and Fleury was as good as any of them. "They had twelve first round draft picks on that team," he recalls. "It opened a lot of eyes of people who'd doubted me. If I could be one of the best twenty juniors in the country I figured I at least deserved to be drafted."

The Tasmanian Devil didn't change his buzzsaw

style at the World Championship. Instead, he turned it up a notch. He started a war by firing the first cheap shot in what would turn out to be Canada's last game. He jumped on the back of a Soviet player fighting one of Fleury's teammates. The benches cleared and the next twenty minutes became the darkest moment in the history of international hockey. Literally. Players were fighting all over the ice. It didn't stop until tournament officials finally had the sense to turn out the lights. Canada and the Soviet Union were both kicked out of the tournament.

How did the man who started it all feel? Thrilled. He enjoyed every minute of it. He returned from Czechoslovakia publicly apologizing for the incident but privately delighted that he'd proven to himself that he could play with the best.

The Calgary Flames weren't as convinced but they were impressed by Fleury's exciting style and showmanship. They thought his flair and size, or lack of same, would create a lot of excitement and interest and help boost attendance at their farm

FLEURY

team in Salt Lake City. That was the main reason they drafted him in the 9th round in 1987. There were 165 players taken ahead of him. Disappointed but not depressed, Fleury returned to Moose Jaw to finish off his junior career. In addition to sharing the scoring lead, Fleury refined the feistiness that would make the NHL think twice about his potential. He had an astounding 235 minutes in penalties, the kind of statistic that could offset concern about his size.

He returned to the next year's World Junior Championships and helped Canada win the gold medal. Late in the season he signed a contract with the Flames and reported to Salt Lake City in time for the playoffs. He quickly proved he could succeed at that level as well, scoring 11 goals in 8 playoff games. By now his confidence had turned to cockiness, sometimes the badge of courage of the small man. The chip on his shoulder had grown into a two-by-four. He told anyone who would listen that he was going to be a star. The Flames weren't as certain. They sent him to Salt Lake City

again. It took him just 40 games to prove

FLEURY

he didn't belong there. He scored 37 goals and 81 points in just 40 games. Big numbers that won him a quick promotion to the big leagues for the second half of the season.

The Flames still regarded him as an experiment, an amusing sideshow. How long before he self-destructed? How long before some big guy pounded on the top of his helmet and drove him through the ice? They soon found out that the answer may be never. As he'd done all his career Fleury used his stick and his speed as the great equalizers. He was a tornado that blew in, wreaked havoc and then was gone just as quickly, leaving victims wondering what had hit them.

His first coach in Calgary, the ebullient Terry Crisp, had made a pro career out of hard work and persistence and he saw a little of himself in the little guy who played until he was exhausted and then played some more. "He reminds me of Ken Linseman, and there's a little Bobby Clarke in him too," said Crisp after Fleury made his debut. "And he also reminds me of Henri Richard, the way he bounces off hits to get up and score."

But he wasn't the second coming of Linseman, Clarke or Richard—he was the first coming of Theoren Fleury. The little guy who looked like the team mascot quickly moved up from the fourth line to the power play. The extra ice time led to more points which led to more ice time until the cycle spun him toward the top of the team scoring race. In his first 36 games in the NHL he scored 34 points, including 14 goals.

By his second year Fleury had become the Cal-gary team leader in every way. His abrasive cockiness off and on the ice made him almost as unpopular with his teammates as with all the other teams in the league. His teammates resented his suggestion that they weren't trying as hard as he was. They weren't, of course. Who could? He became the measuring stick for NHL intensity. He got twice as many votes as anyone else in a league-wide poll that named him the Hardest Working Player in the league. Teammate Al MacInnis admitted, "He hasn't made a lot of friends in the league. But he's a quality player and he means a lot to us."

Fleury doesn't apologize or plan to change the style that has given him success at every level of hockey. He was named the 1987–'88 Major Junior Player of the Year by the *The Hockey News;* he was part of the gold-medal-winning Canadian Junior team in 1988 plus helped the Salt Lake City Golden Eagles win the International Hockey League championship; he won the Stanley Cup with the Flames in 1989; and, during the 1990–'91 season, he became the smallest player in NHL history to score 50 goals (51) in one season.

"A big part of my game is intensity," he says. If I don't play intensely I don't feel like I'm doing my job. That's everybody's responsibility, to do their jobs." And that's all he has wanted to do his whole life—to prove that size has nothing to do with getting a job done. Theoren Fleury stands taller than anyone else when you look for players who symbolize those two qualities NHL coaches treasure above all others—intensity and desire. ★

Jaromir Jagr

It's early summer in Vancouver. The beaches at English Bay are jammed with sun worshippers desperately trying to squeeze every minute out of a sun they know could disappear behind clouds and not emerge for weeks in this soggy climate. The bay is alive with a sea of white sails dancing on top of the waves. The tennis courts in Stanley Park are bouncing with life. The city's golf courses are crowded. Everywhere you look people are playing. Everywhere except in a dark room on Renfrew Street where half a dozen men are working feverishly, watching video tape, trying to read between the lines of scouting reports, arguing about the strengths and weaknesses of kids barely old enough to drive.

The Vancouver Canucks long ago ended another miserable season of hockey. In the third year of their latest New Era, Pat Quinn's team had finished a dismal 20th out of 21 teams. Only Quebec was worse. But misery does have its rewards in the NHL. The Canucks will have the second pick in the upcoming draft. A draft that will be held in Vancouver. A draft that will mine one of the richest veins of talent in a decade.

JAGR

The Canucks' brain trust is in a dilemma. They know Quebec will almost certainly take a big, powerful winger from the Ontario Hockey League, Owen Nolan. The Vancouver scouts are pushing for the hulking Kevin Primeau who led the OHL in scoring in the season just finished. They also like the mature, steady though unspectacular play of Mike Ricci, the captain of both the Peterborough Petes and Canada's champi-

onship World Junior team. Pat Quinn and **JAGR** his Director of Hockey Operations, Brian Burke, aren't satisfied with any of those. They're looking for the franchise player, the 50 goal, 100 point man the Canucks have never had.

It comes down to a choice between Seattle's exciting Gretzky clone—Petr Nedved—or the virtually unknown Jaromir Jagr. Like Nedved, Jagr is from Czechoslovakia. Unlike Nedved, Jagr is still

in Czechoslovakia. He did not defect. It was that patriotism that finally forced the Canucks to forget Jagr. The outspoken Burke acknowledged it could have been a major mistake. "Jagr's the most talented player in the draft. He's the one player that could step in and be an impact player right away," said Burke. "But it could be years before the Czechs release him, and we can't wait."

A few days later a full house in the Pacific Coliseum gave Quinn a standing ovation when he announced the Canucks had drafted Nedved immediately after Quebec had taken Nolan. Detroit selecting third went with Primeau and Philadelphia drafting fourth took Ricci. Twenty minutes after the draft started, Pittsburgh General Manager Craig Patrick could finally relax. For twenty minutes he'd been afraid one of the other teams would take a chance on Jagr. With a relieved smile he announced Pittsburgh would use the 5th pick to take the man they'd rated number one in the draft, Jaromir Jagr, an 18 year old from Kladno, Czechoslovakia. The Penguins felt they had the steal of the draft. Burke was afraid they were right. He just hoped they'd have as much trouble signing Jagr as everyone expected.

They didn't, because the times they were a changin' in Eastern Europe. Jagr was the first Czechoslovakian to attend an NHL draft without having to defect. What scared off the rest of the NHL was his military obligations and fears that his club, Kladno, would hold Jagr for ransom. The 18 year old was already a big star in his hometown. He led them in scoring with 30 goals, 30 assists and 60 points in 51 games. The 6' 2", 200-pounder was considered by many to be the best player to come out of Czechoslovakia since Peter Stastny. Unlike the Stastnys or Nedved, Jagr was not going to leave his homeland illegally. He still had a year left on his contract with Kladno, plus the military obligations which could keep him out of the NHL for another two or three years.

The Penguins needed a lot of luck to sign Jagr and they got it. The entire East Bloc collapsed that summer. The Berlin Wall came down and when training camp opened that fall the Penguins had bought out Kladno and Jagr was an NHLer.

Pittsburgh did its best to make the transition as comfortable as possible. They found a Czechoslovakian family for him to live with in a suburb of Pittsburgh. They paid for Berlitz courses to help him learn English. But like so many Europeans before him, Jagr still felt lost and alone.

The first wave of Europeans in the NHL were mature young men in their mid-to-late twenties. They'd travelled and played away from home all their lives. North America was just one big, extended road trip. Jagr was still a boy, going through all the usual trauma of youngsters who leave home for the first time. Jagr's problems were twice as painful because the new language did not come easily to him.

Contrary to the opinion of Brian Burke and other sharp-eyed NHL bird-dogs, Jaromir Jagr did not look ready to play in the NHL. He showed occasional flashes and rushes of brilliance but he couldn't seem to finish anything off. By the middle of December, two and a half months into the season, he seemed to be getting worse, not better. In one 15 game period that stretched out over nearly a month, Jagr had one single, solitary point—an assist. Worst of all, the youngster expected to create so many scoring chances had only 12 shots on goal in 15 games. Even Coach Bob Johnson's remarkable patience was being strained to the limit.

General Manager Craig Patrick astutely recognized that Jagr's problems on the ice were merely symptomatic of his larger adjustment off the ice. "He was homesick," Patrick explains. "He couldn't understand the language and he was getting depressed. He was trying but it's hard to get along with your teammates if you can't understand what they're talking about." The general manager solved the problem quite easily. He went out and found someone for Jagr to talk to. In a trade, he picked up a 31-year-old Czechoslovakian, Jiri Hrdina, from Calgary.

The change was obvious immediately. Jagr's black mood lifted. He was smiling and he was scoring again. No goals and one assist in the month before Hrdina's arrival. Six goals and nine assists in the month after he arrived in Pittsburgh. Revived and relaxed, Jagr went on to finish fourth in rookie scoring with 27 goals and 30 assists for 57 points. Coach Johnson described the trade as the turning point in Jagr's career. "He needed someone to talk with even if it was just about the weather," he said.

JAGR

"He thought scoring goals was everything. Trying too hard, it started to get him down, even in practise."

His new linemate, the veteran Bryan Trottier, also saw the homesick kid evolve slowly into a bright, young star. "He improved every day after the trade," observed Trottier. "He's so big and strong. He surprises a lot of people in the corner."

Surprise is a word that's used a lot to describe Jagr. It's easy to be fooled by his baby face. You don't expect that kind of size and strength from someone who looks younger than your paper boy. He's surprisingly strong and determined in the corners. You don't expect that from a high-scoring star. His straight-backed, almost stiff-legged style of skating produces speed that catches a lot of players by surprise. Most surprising of all are the subtle weight shifts and the Lemieux-like reach that produce dekes that shock and embarrass NHL defensemen. It earned him the nickname—The Human Highlight Reel.

A surprising (there's that word again) number of his goals are brilliant one-on-one or one-on-three solo rushes that leave a trail of twisted bodies and broken pride behind him. The goal that will live forever in the video history of the Penguin's first Stanley Cup championship came at a crucial time for Pittsburgh. After winning the first division title in their history, the Penguins were in danger of quickly giving away home-ice advantage in the first round of the playoffs. New Jersey took the opening game 3 to 1, and was within one lucky bounce of taking two in a row. The Stanley Cup might never have wound up in Pittsburgh if Jagr hadn't taken the game and destiny in his own hands.

He took a pass from Phil Bourque and glided over the blueline. The Devil's John MacLean came across to check Jagr but the kid casually held him off with one arm. He got a step ahead of MacLean and then surprised goaltender Chris Terreri with that amazing reach of his, sliding the puck from backhand to forehand and flipping it over a falling Terreri. All that with one hand on the stick! At 8:52 of overtime, Jaromir Jagr wins it for Pittsburgh, 5 to 4. They go on to eliminate the stubborn Devils in seven games. That was as close as they came to losing en route to their first Stanley Cup. Jagr set some rookie scoring records including five assists in the six games of the final series.

In his first season Jagr proved the Canucks were right. They would live to regret not drafting Jagr. While Nedved struggled Jagr was head and broad shoulders above everyone taken in the 1990 draft. The Human Highlight Reel amazed and delighted fans and teammates in Pittsburgh. Kevin Stevens said, "He's so pretty to watch. Thank God we got him." Mario Lemieux gave the ultimate praise from a high source when he said, "His reach is fantastic. He skates so well. He can score goals and he's even started to control the game a little bit. Best of all he's only 19."

In his second year Jagr continued to thrill fans and scare defensemen with his thrilling rushes. He made the all-star team and continued to score at his rookie pace. Like most young scoring stars Jagr is mesmerized by the puck and often forgets to pick up his man until it's too late. He worked harder on those defensive responsibilities in his sophomore season and the results showed in a dramatically improved plus–minus rating. He's also working on improving a shot that's the weakest part of his game. He doesn't have the gift of the Midas touch around the net that makes scoring superstars out of players with otherwise average ability, players like Steve Larmer and Michel Goulet. Most of their goals are forgettable tap-ins or tip-ins. It's hard to forget any goal scored by Jaromir Jagr. The Human Highlight Reel may never score 50 goals but he'll get 30 a year that you'll remember for a lifetime.

There's a moment in every young star's life when the opportunity finally arrives for him to rise to greatness or settle back into the long line of players with exceptional physical talent who never reach their potential.

That moment arrived for Jaromir Jagr in the spring of 1992. It wasn't a moment, it was one sickening second. The New York Rangers' Adam Graves swung his stick like an axe and chopped down a giant—Mario Lemieux. Graves turned his stick so that the heel hit Lemieux on the back of the hand, breaking a bone. Graves was suspended for the rest of the playoffs but Lemieux would also miss the rest of the Patrick division final.

It was a bitter battle between the top teams in the league, the Rangers and the defending Stanley Cup champions from Pittsburgh. Most experts wrote the Penguins off after they lost Lemieux. They didn't realize that Pittburgh still had Lethal

JAGR

Weapon 2 in reserve, a Lemieux clone named Jaromir Jagr.

The youngster seized the moment of greatness with the series tied at two games apiece. Jagr was brilliant, using his surprising strength and remarkable shiftiness to score two of the Penguins' three goals in New York. The Penguins 3–2 victory gave them control of the series. The Rangers were finished but Jagr was just beginning. Pittsburgh returned home to complete the elimination of the Rangers in six games.

Lemieux returned for the Prince of Wales division final with Boston, but Jagr was still the star. The overmatched, overachieving Boston Bruins got great goaltending from Andy Moog and their characteristic hard work from the lunch-bucket brigade and forced game one into overtime. That's when Jagr went to work. He scored a brilliant goal, stickhandling and sideslipping through nearly the entire Bruin team to score his fourth game-winning goal of the playoffs, his third in three games. Even Marvelous Mario Lemieux had never seen anything like it. "He's such a great player," said Lemieux. "He's so strong in the upper body and he handles the puck so well. It's fun just to watch him."

Jagr returned the compliment. He learned many of his great moves by watching Mario who he jokingly referred to as his Dad. Jagr's performance in the playoffs astounded no one more than his teammates. They could only look at Jagr and marvel. Defenseman Gord Roberts admitted, "I am very jealous of Jagr. To be 20, to be so big and strong, to be able to do the things he can do—how can you not be jealous?" Added Rick Tocchet, "He's just a big kid who's having the time of his life."

Jagr dedicated the playoffs to another big influence in his life, Bob Johnson. After leading the Penguins to the Stanley Cup a year before, the popular coach had fallen victim, and subsequently died, of a brain tumor. He was gone but his influence lived on. "He will always be number one forever for me," said Jagr.

The kid became a teen idol overnight with his brilliant play, baby face and long curls. He told a reporter he loved a certain kind of chocolate bar, Kit-Kats, and he got hundreds of them from fans. "I get a thousand of them," he said. What did he do with them? "I eat them all," he admitted, with the look of a kid who'd cleaned out the cookie jar.

Defensemen who tried to keep up with him on the ice weren't surprised to learn he loved to go fast everywhere he went. "I get a hundred speeding tickets this year," he confessed. "I get three in one week. They don't care if I'm a hero." Maybe not, but almost everyone else in Pittsburgh certainly does. The city fell head over heels for the innocent from abroad. His coming-out party ended with a four-game sweep of the Bruins and the Blackhawks. With 23 points, including 10 goals in 20 games he finished fourth in playoff scoring behind teammates Lemieux, Francis and Stevens.

Pittsburgh won its second straight Stanley Cup.

JAGR

"What's so hard about this?" Jagr joked. "I win Stanley Cup every year I'm in the league." With Mario One and Mario Two, Pittsburgh may keep on winning every year Jagr stays in the league. The best player in the world, number 66, Lemieux, looked at number 68, Jagr, and said proudly, "He has all the tools to be the best player in the world one day."

One day when Lemieux retires. Jagr is in no rush. He just wants to keep on winning and most importantly of all, to keep on having fun. There's only one thing he wants to change: "Maybe I get fewer speeding tickets!" ★

Joe Juneau

Joe Juneau, one of the hottest young stars during the 1992 Albertville Olympics, was drafted almost as an afterthought by Boston in 1988. He was the 81st player taken. At that time, the native of Pont-Rouge, Quebec was more concerned about making it through university than making it to the NHL.

JUNEAU

He'd been recruited by RPI—Rennselaer Polytechnic Institute—in upstate New York, not far from his Quebec home. He was an excellent student all through his French high school, but his English was only at the grade one level. Even though U.S. colleges have a reputation for giving star athletes a free academic ride to their degree, Juneau had to work hard on his English and his studies. There weren't any classes in Basket Weaving or Hockey 101. But Juneau proved how dedicated a student he was, graduating with a degree in Aeronautical Engineering, as well as near-flawless English.

Juneau was also an honours student in hockey. RPI was a hockey powerhouse that had already sent Adam Oates to the NHL. Juneau was faster and trickier, a much better skater than Oates. He challenged all of Oates' college scoring records but was still a longshot to make it in the NHL. Until, that is, he started studying under the guru of international hockey, Dave King.

Juneau joined the Canadian team preparing for the Olympics and by the time he arrived in Albertville he was the leading scorer and most exciting player on the team. An old teammate at RPI, Tony Hejna, watched him sparkle on TV and said incredulously, "It's unbelievable how much better he's become since he left here last year." Juneau confirmed the improvement and gave King all the credit: "He made me a lot better player. After a year of playing and practising with the Canadian team I learned a lot. I'm definitely a lot better than I was when I came out of college."

The larger ice surface and free-wheeling hockey were perfect for the speedy Juneau. He had the quickness around the outside and the tricky spin moves inside that were reminiscent of a young Denis Savard. Juneau led all Olympic scorers with 11 points in five games including an unforgettable goal against Czechoslovakia. He appeared to be skating in high speed but some-

JUNEAU

how found another gear and shifted into overdrive, slipping between the two defensemen. When one of them tried desperately to haul him down, Juneau held him off with one arm and still managed to scoop the puck into the net. One of the fans in Albertville standing and applauding with amazement was Harry Sinden. He was excited about the Bruins prospect but also realized that each goal was going to cost him a fortune—Juneau had already turned down half a dozen offers from the Bruins.

The brilliant student was bright enough to realize he was in the perfect bargaining position. "I still want to complete my Masters degree," he said. "I'm

four courses short and it means almost as much to me as hockey. But at the moment hockey is the only thing on my mind." And he certainly had lots of options. His thrilling rushes in the Olympics had made him an overnight sensation in Europe. He had offers from the Italian and Swiss leagues that would pay him almost as well as the Bruins and also give him the time he needed to finish off his Masters degree. But his biggest bargaining weapon turned out to be the Swedish assassin, Ulf Samuelsson. The infamously wicked and sneaky Swede had caught Bruin's superstar Cam Neely with his head down a year earlier in the Stanley Cup playoffs. He hit him with a knee that drove so deep into Neely's thigh that it caused the bone to calcify. Neely would need a year to recover and even then his career and future appeared doubtful.

Without Neely the Bruins had fallen far behind the division-leading Montreal Canadiens. With plans for a newer and bigger Boston Garden nearing completion the Bruins needed someone to ignite their attack and turn on the fans. Juneau was the spark plug. Harry Sinden, the Uncle Scrooge of NHL general managers, finally relented and gave Juneau the guaranteed one-way pro contract he wanted.

Dave King felt that no matter what the Bruins paid they were getting a bargain: "He's a hard worker which makes him a natural in Boston. He's a good goal-scorer and an intelligent passer." Juneau had finished his college career at RPI second in overall scoring to the man they called

JUNEAU

Adam Assist. Oates was one of the finest passers in the game. He was now also a Bruin, picked up in a late-season trade with St. Louis.

It didn't take Juneau long to make himself at home in Boston. He moved in with a couple of other college kids who were new Bruins, Ted Donato and Steve Heinze. He also managed to fit in comfortably on the ice. His zip put some much-needed punch in the Bruins' lineup. He scored 5 goals and used that superb passing Dave King had talked about to set up 14 other goals—19 points in just 14 games. After struggling to hang on in the Adams division, Boston put a late-season charge on Montreal, before finally settling back to finish a strong second.

Juneau continued his productivity in the '92 playoffs. He was the Bruins second-leading scorer as they beat-out the Sabres in seven games and then stunned the Canadiens in four games to win the division in a sweep. Tiring late in the longest season of his life, Juneau lost his jump in the Stanley Cup semi-finals against Pittsburgh, and the Bruins were defeated by the eventual Cup winners. Juneau capped off his incredible introduction into the NHL by being the rookie playoff scoring leader.

"Personally, I feel great about my first year," he said. "I gained a lot of confidence this year thanks to Dave King, and I carried it over to the Bruins."

And Boston had seen enough to realize that with the aeronautical engineer in their lineup they could start working on plans to fly even higher in the future. ★

Brian Leetch

The accidental twists and turns in Brian Leetch's life took him to New York to play for the Rangers. He could just as easily have been playing for another team of Rangers in his native state of Texas. Instead of trying to end the New York Rangers half-century-long Stanley Cup jinx, Brian Leetch could just as easily have been helping the Expos or Blue Jays end their own playoff jinx.

Leetch was born in Corpus Christi, Texas and grew up with a baseball in his hand. He loved baseball but when his family moved to the Boston area, Leetch discovered another love of his life—hockey. But he continued to play baseball in the summer. By his senior year in high school he'd grown into a Tom Seaver clone: 5' 11", 190 pounds. Barrel-chested with a lively arm that could fire a fastball at 90 miles per hour. He struck out 19 batters in one high school game, breaking a record set by Juan Nieves who went on to a career in the major leagues.

There was no question that Leetch had a major-league arm. If he'd concentrated on baseball and become even a borderline starter in the majors he'd be making twice as much money as he gets for being one of the best defensemen in the NHL. But he has no regrets. "One bad pitch, you throw your arm out and you're done," he says, and candidly adds: "I'm not going to hit any home runs or anything so that would be it for me. I just like the team aspect of hockey a lot more, moving the puck and so on. I'd like to think now that I could have done something in baseball, but who can say?"

LEETCH

What we can say after four years in the NHL is that Brian Leetch made the **LEETCH** to adjust to the permanent change to defense. His goal-scoring fell from 40 in his last year in high school to nine in his only year in college. He still managed to produce 47 points in 37 games and was chosen Hockey East Player of the Year and Rookie of the Year. During his Christmas break he played for the United States team at the World Junior Championships.

right choice. If his dad hadn't transferred to New England the NHL might never have enjoyed the skills of the player destined to be the dominant defenseman of the '90s. Like many NHLers, Brian Leetch comes from an athletic family. His sister Beth became a long distance runner, competing in the Boston marathon. Brian was consumed by hockey. He quickly developed into a high school all star. At 16 he scored 30 goals and added 46 assists for a total of 76 points in just 26 games. His senior year he was even better, getting 40 goals, 44 assists and 84 points in 28 games. Leetch was an easy choice as MVP for his second straight year at Avon Old Farms high school. He was named New England Prep School Player of the Year, beating out Jeremy Roenick at rival Thayer Academy.

The NHL was a bit gun-shy about picking American high school kids too early in the draft after the Brian Lawton fiasco. Lawton was the first player chosen in the 1983 draft, taken ahead of future stars like Pat LaFontaine and Steve Yzerman. Minnesota had drafted purely out of patriotism and paid for it. Lawton was a disappointment and drifted around the NHL with six teams before finally settling in with the expansion San Jose Sharks.

The circumstances and coincidences that shaped Leetch's life were at work again. If not for the past failures of Lawton and other U.S. prep school stars, Leetch would have been one of the first two or three players taken. He would never have been around when New York drafted 9th in 1986. They snapped him up. The Rangers general manager Neil Smith was Detroit's chief scout when the Rangers drafted Leetch in '86. He felt Leetch had a lot to learn about the defensive side of the game. That's why he'd recommended Detroit take Joe Murphy with its first choice in the draft. Smith added that "Brian had to learn how to handle the physical side of the game. He took too many risks with the puck and got himself into too much trouble." That was understandable for a player who'd been a forward for most of his high school career.

Now converted to a rushing defenseman, he was in no rush to play in the NHL. He didn't feel he was ready and passed up the Rangers offer to spend a valuable year at Boston College. It gave him time

This wonderful taste of international hockey left him yearning for more. He dropped out of college the next year to play for the U.S. Olympic team. His maturity and poise made him a leader on and off the ice. Although he was only 19 he was made captain of a veteran team of Americans, and his strong play led them to a near-upset of the powerful Soviet team at the 1988 Calgary Olympics. He had also played in the World Junior Championships for the third straight year, and was named to the first team all-stars. The Rangers didn't have to wait any more. He joined them for the last month of the regular season. The transition was painless; he quickly raised his game to the NHL level. His quickness and powerful skating produced 14 points in those final 17 games.

Roger Neilson, a quiet unflappable coach, doesn't get excited about too many things but he was thrilled with the way Leetch took control of the power play. "He stepped in and right away you expected him to play half the game, pick the team

up when it's down, run the power play, **LEETCH** and without any fanfare it just happened. Handling a superstar can be difficult," says Neilson, "but with Brian we just let him play."

That's because Brian Leetch doesn't think of himself as a superstar—never has, never will. "I've had good years," says Leetch, "but there's a lot of work to do to be considered with the Coffeys and Bourques. Al MacInnis has come close. Stevens, Hatcher and other guys like that have done it for so long and come through in the clutch. I'd like to be in that category some day, but I've got a lot of work to do till then."

Not as much as he thinks. His skating is strong and deceptively quick. With his square, tank-like build he appears to be moving a lot slower than he actually is. He's the best in the league at penetrating from the point. His shot is low and hard but when forecheckers try to pressure him he moves laterally in huge strides that seem to cover ten or fifteen feet. He plants an edge and almost rockets the other way without losing any speed. He's alone in front and with his head up he quickly picks out an opening or slides a clever pass to a wide-open teammate. His defensive partner, David Shaw, chuckles as he recalls some of the more incredible goals Leetch has produced: "His lateral movement is unbelieveable. You say to yourself, 'How'd he do that?'" Roger Neilson adds, "When he makes one of his moves the only people in the rink who aren't left in shock are the guys on the bench. We've all seen him do it night after night."

The moves add up to record-breaking numbers. He beat Barry Beck's NHL record for goals by a rookie defenseman, scoring 22 on his way to the Calder Trophy as Rookie of the Year in 1988–'89. His second season his numbers went down and so did he in a corner of Maple Leaf Gardens. He broke his ankle late in the season in Toronto. "It ruined my summer but otherwise it never bothered me again," he sighs with relief. "In fact it inspired me to get in the best shape of my life. If anything, my legs are stronger than ever."

Any doubts about his durability quickly disappeared. He became the only Ranger to play all 80 games in the 1990–'91 season. He broke Brad Park's club record for points by a defenseman with 88. He also took care of Mike Roger's Ranger record for assists with 72. Park wasn't surprised at losing his record to Leetch. "He does a lot of the same things I did," says Park, "such as holding the puck at the point longer to suck people in, and then moving it quickly and accurately to the open man. Bourque and Coffey are getting older. Leetch is the best young guy on the block. There's no doubt in my mind."

Prophetic words. In 1991–'92 Leetch emerged as the new king of the blueline. He led the Rangers to first place in the toughest division in the league, the Patrick. They also finished first in the league standings for the first time in nearly half a century. General Manager Neil Smith, who'd worried about Leetch earlier in his career, was learning to relax. "Brian is a dazzling risk-taker," he explains. "He does things that make you jump out of your chair if they work. And most of the time they do."

Leetch gave an incredible demonstration of what Smith was talking about late in the season in a game against Philadelphia. He swooped into the corner to the right of the Rangers' goal, scooped up the puck and in one daring move broke the golden rule of hockey—never cut in front of your own net. He swept in front of a shocked John Vanbiesbrouck and an equally thunderstruck Flyer forechecker. He left them both behind in a dazzling burst of speed that carried him to the centre of the ice. A quick fake, and an even quicker shift, left a couple more Flyers in his wake. He swept in over the blueline with only one man to beat. He faked right, went left and buried his left blade in the ice, a move that made him seem to pick up speed in the change of direction. The defenseman, Mark Howe, was left behind as Leetch hurtled across in front of Ron Hextall. The goaltender tried desperately to poke-check the puck away, but Leetch brought it closer to his body and then calmly flipped it into the open net.

It was the kind of goal you see only in dreams and movies. He'd skated through the entire team and scored the goal of the year. It was the most stunning of the 22 goals he scored that season. He joined the legends—Orr, Coffey, Potvin and MacInnis—as the only defensemen to score a hundred points in a season. It earned him his first Norris Trophy as NHL Defenseman of the Year. It proved Brian Leetch had finally arrived. He was the defenseman of the '90s whether he wanted to admit it or not. ★

Niklas Lidstrom

If they'd stopped the 1991–'92 season at Christmas and handed out the awards, Detroit's Niklas Lidstrom would have been a unanimous choice as Rookie of the Year. His NHL career got off to a super start. But that was hardly a surprise to Detroit coach Bryan Murray. He'd watched him quarterback Sweden to the World Championship in the spring of 1991. "He was so good on the power play it was scary," bubbles Murray. "We all knew he was going to be unbelievable because he sees the ice so well, passes great and has great offensive skills. He plays a poised game and has outstanding ability to pass and shoot the puck. He is just a very skillful player."

He should be. He went to school to learn hockey. The youngster from Vasteras, Sweden was a superb natural athlete with excellent hand-eye coordination. He was good at all sports but he loved hockey more than anything else. Lots of kids go to hockey school in the summer. Lidstrom went to hockey school all winter. He was actually educated in hockey.

LIDSTROM

"In high school," he explained, "I took a class in hockey. We studied **LIDSTROM** the game and practised drills for five hours a week." With that fully-rounded education behind him Lidstrom quickly graduated magna cum laude to the Swedish Elite League when he was only 17. He played three years for his town club of Vasteras. Even though he never scored more than 8 goals or 16 points in any season he was attracting more and more attention from scouts in the NHL.

Christer Rockstrom, a European bird dog for the Detroit Red Wings, was impressed by Lidstrom's precocious play on the point on power plays. Detroit's head scout, Neil Smith (who later moved on to become General Manager of the New York Rangers), agreed with Rockstrom's prediction that Lidstrom could be one of the few European defensemen who could make the transformation to the NHL.

The wider ice surface in Europe changes the criteria for defensemen. It puts more emphasis on speed and skating, instead of the size and toughness that are the two biggest prerequisites for NHL defensemen. Borje Salming and Stefan Persson, two of Lidstrom's boyhood idols in Sweden, were two of the few European defensemen who made the transition and were true stars in the NHL. Salming played 17 Hall-of-Fame seasons with Toronto and then finished his career with a year in Detroit in 1989–'90. After the Red Wings drafted Lidstrom in the third round in 1989, Salming met the youngster and assured him he could play in the NHL. "He helped me a lot," says a grateful Lidstrom, "especially by warning me the schedule would be the hardest part of the first year."

Salming's words would echo through Lidstrom's mind often during the long, exhausting winter months to come. Hockey is an enervating game. Off-days are often spent travelling instead of resting. And when you're as good as Lidstrom the season is even longer because you're invited to play for your country in international play. Turning down the invitation would be sensible but unpatriotic. The 40-game schedule with Vastaras didn't come close to preparing him for the busiest year of his life.

Lidstrom was the heart of a swift, mobile defense that helped Sweden win the World Championships in the spring of '91. He also played a key role in the team that made it to the semi-finals at the Canada Cup a couple of short months later. Murray, who coached Canada at the World Championships, recalls that "Lidstrom was on the ice all the time. He

was one of the best defencemen in **LIDSTROM** He'd played more than 90 games during 1991. His play lacked the zip it had in the first half. But he was still making the best breakout passes in the league. One teammate estimated Lidstrom had created more than a dozen breakaways for the Red Wings in barely half a season.

the tournament. He scored a couple of goals against the Americans on point shots that were so low and hard that John Vanbiesbrouck (goalie for the New York Rangers) never saw them coming."

The Red Wings knew Lidstrom was the point man who could solve their problems with a power play that was pathetic for a team with so much talent up front. Detroit's power play was third worst in the league in 1990–'91. That sorry statistic spurred the Red Wings to buy out Lidstrom's contract with his Swedish team. They felt that $300,000 was a small price to pay for improving the worst part of the team's game.

They handed Lidstrom a steady job on defense and wisely paired him with stay-at-home specialist Brad McCrimmon. They wound up with the best plus-minus rating of any defensive pairing in the league, and they finished second (McCrimmon +39) and third (Lidstrom +36) in the league's final plus-minus standings. Only teammate Paul Ysebaert was better with a league-leading +44. Ysebaert was impressed by Lidstrom's quiet efficiency: "He doesn't say much. He's not flashy. But he's consistent night after night."

After Christmas the effects of the long schedule, the travel, and the summer of playing in both a World Championship and a Canada Cup, finally caught up with him. He hit the wall, fading badly.

Defensively, he was still solid, but his scoring fell off. It cost him the Calder Cup. Steady Tony Amonte took over the rookie scoring lead that Lidstrom had held for the first few months. Lidstrom would eventually finish fourth in the rookie scoring derby. He had been named NHL Rookie of the Month in both November and December, but he didn't win it again.

The Calder became a race between Amonte and Vancouver's explosive Pavel Bure, but Lidstrom was one of the finalists. He was also happy about his position on the Red Wings, where he was third in plus-minus, 6th in team scoring with 11 goals, 49 assists and 60 points.

He was also number one with coach Bryan Murray. "Niklas played a lot and he played well. He is what we thought he would be, one of the best young defensemen to come into the league in years." No one could ask for more in one year. He'll never be as dashing or daring as a Bourque or Coffey but the silent Swede will be a solid part of the Red Wings defense of the '90s. ★

Trevor Linden

It's the eyes that signal the subtle difference between good and great. It's the eyes you can't see when you study the clinical statistics that measure an athlete's career. On paper, Trevor Linden may never reach the mileposts of greatness—50 goals and 130 points in a season. But if you could see "the look," you'd understand why coaches and opponents won't be surprised if Linden's gargantuan strides someday carry him straight into the Hall of Fame.

LINDEN

You can see "the look" on Linden's *Young Superstars* hockey card put out by Score early in his third season. Cold, piercing, ignoring the camera and other distractions of life in the spotlight, glaring straight ahead toward the hated enemy. It's the look of hockey from the '30s, '40s and '50s. Trevor Linden is a throwback to the days when the hated enemy was a reality, not a cliché. The days when hockey was war, not just a game.

They came off the cold prairies and out of harsh mining towns in Ontario and Quebec, playing for peanuts yet fighting with their lives against anyone trying to steal those peanuts. They truly believed there was no difference in talent, only in desire and dedication. Trevor Linden truly believes, "To this day, I don't think I'm blessed with talent. I've had to work for everything I've got."

His coach for the first two years of his NHL career, Bob McCammon, credits Linden's parents with turning out a good old-fashioned boy with good old-fashioned values. "They believed in hard work" he says, "and that's a big reason for his success." His mother reveals it was more than that. "Trevor was always more competitive," she says. "He had to win at everything he did."

The precociousness and determination

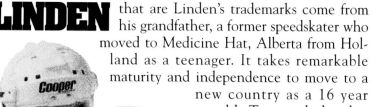

LINDEN

that are Linden's trademarks come from his grandfather, a former speedskater who moved to Medicine Hat, Alberta from Holland as a teenager. It takes remarkable maturity and independence to move to a new country as a 16 year old. Trevor shakes his head in amazement and admiration for his grandfather Nick: "He's a great old guy. He never started anything he didn't finish. One day he was working on the farm and the tractor flipped over on him. He got his legs trapped under a smokestack. Doctors thought he might not survive, but he was determined to see his first grandson (Trevor's older brother), and that determination pulled him through."

In 1949 Nick Linden started the gravel and construction companies that would become the foundation of the family's financial success. His son, Trevor's dad, took over the company and showed the same Dutch stubbornness and determination to keep it alive during the financially rough years ahead. "He did it by sheer hard work," boasts a proud Trevor. "That's probably the biggest thing my dad and granddad taught me."

The three generations of Lindens still work hard to keep the business and their family farm running near Medicine Hat. Each June the family gets together for branding. The kids wrestle the calves into submission, while granddad Nick brands them. A couple of days of fighting with 300-pound calves can make a year of wrestling with 200-pound NHLers seem like child's play. "I love to get back every summer," says Linden. "It's a place that will always be home to me."

Medicine Hat was where the boy and his dreams were born. Hockey wasn't a love, it was a passion from the day when a four year old eagerly pressured his dad into taking him to the outdoor rink. His dad tried to talk sense into little Trevor. After all, it was 40 below outside. But that famous Linden stubbornness and determination persevered. He'd just received his first NHL sweater and was ready to get started! His father finally relented, drove him to the rink and then sat in the warmth of his car watching Trevor skate for hours, living out the fantasy he was convinced would become a reality someday.

It would take a lot of years and a lot of driving to the rink for the Lindens to help their three sons live out their dreams. His older brother Dean worked for, but did not play with the Medicine Hat Tigers. Jamie, three years younger than Trevor, would one day play with the Spokane Chiefs, also in the Western Hockey League. The only time it was quiet in the Linden household was when Hockey Night In Canada came on TV. Naturally the kids fantasized about playing in the NHL, but Trevor's dreams were more modest. "I always loved the NHL but my real goal was to play for the Medicine Hat Tigers," he reveals.

The Linden boys spent their winters on the ice, their summers in the backyard. "We had a net and we'd shoot at that thing for hours," he remembers. Trevor's climb up the minor league ladder in "the Hat" was slowed by only one person, his mother. "Trevor's headstrong. I had to keep him away from practise a few times when he was eleven because he lost his temper in a game. That taught him a lesson but he's still very strong-willed," says Mom.

Linden chuckles and admits Mom is right. "I've always been a sore loser," he says. "The worst thing she'd do to me was not let me play the next game. Anything else would have been okay. I banged my stick on the boards once and she wouldn't let me play the next game. By the time I was twelve I'd learned my lesson." With his mother helping him focus his drive into positive channels plus the long hours in the backyard and on the rink helping his skating and shooting, Linden achieved the goal he'd dreamed about.

He graduated to the Medicine Hat Tigers when he was fifteen. "I grew fast and was nearly my current height (6' 3"). I played 8 or 10 games with

LINDEN

them and then the next year (at 16) I stuck with them for the full year." Like most Alberta boys he idolized Wayne Gretzky, but he wore number 16, a tribute to his real hero, the indefatiguable Bobby Clarke. Russ Farwell, now the General Manager of the Philadelphia Flyers, was in charge of Medicine Hat during Linden's career with the Tigers. "He's got the same work ethic as Clarke," he says, "but I think he may be more talented than Bobby."

The talent was obvious on the ice. The maturity and leadership were equally apparent in the dressing room. He became captain of the Tigers and during the next two seasons led them to back-to-back Memorial Cup championships. Five days after turning 17 he scored two goals in a 6–2 win over Oshawa that won the first national championship in the history of Medicine Hat. In his second full year of junior he scored 46 goals and 110 points, but it was the things he did without the puck that caught the eye of the NHL.

Vancouver had second pick in the 1988 draft and were looking for the franchise player every team needs as a cornerstone. Minnesota would take Mike Modano with the first pick because of his higher scoring and his birth certificate. He was an American who could help draw fans to a struggling franchise. That was perfectly alright with the Canucks. Linden was the one they really wanted. Mike Penny, their chief scout, remembers, "We double-checked everything. We talked to the coaches, the managers, all the people in his life in Medicine Hat. No one ever said a negative word about the kid."

Canuck scouts watched him play more than 30 games. General Manager Pat Quinn loved Linden's single-minded devotion to the game. A journeyman who turned ordinary talent into a nine-year NHL career by hard work, Quinn could relate to the kid who was a throwback to earlier NHL stars. "I especially liked his qualities in the dressing room," says Quinn. "He had leadership as a 15 year old and the ability to deal with and be a leader of 19 and 20 year olds. That's an unusual thing. When Minnesota made Modano the top pick in the 1988 draft, the loudest cheers came from the Canuck table. They had their franchise player. The hard work had paid off. Linden had made the NHL.

What did he do to celebrate that summer? Work harder. He threw himself into an exhausting conditioning program, lifting weights. "I was worn out after the Memorial Cup," he recalls. "My weight had dropped to about 155 pounds on draft day. I knew I had to be a lot heavier than that." He quickly regained his normal weight of 180 and kept on going, bulking up to a muscular 200 pounds by the time hockey season rolled around again.

The fact that he even showed up at training camp was further proof that Linden was a throwback. His agent hadn't been able to work out a contract with the Canucks. Modano had similar problems with Minnesota and never did show up. But there was never any question of a holdout in Linden's mind. He'd have played for nothing. He showed up and despite an understandably nervous, jittery start, quickly proved he could play in the NHL. It was the best bargaining ploy he could have used. Satisfied they had the real thing in Linden, the Canucks signed him to a long-term contract the day before the regular season began.

In a training camp diary published in the *Vancouver Province* newspaper the rookie wrote, "The pace here is faster than junior but about the same as in the World Championship tournament. (Linden played on the Canadian team that won the Gold Medal.) The defensemen are so much bigger. It's the difference between men and boys. But now I'm learning to treat it like just another camp. It's just a matter of settling down and playing my game. We had a motivational meeting with a sports psychologist. He talked to us about visualization, keeping a positive attitude. I'm really into that mental stuff. I think it's very important. So much about the game is attitude. If you can prepare yourself mentally, it's half the battle."

Linden is a warrior, willing to do anything to win the battle. His intensity won him a spot in the starting lineup in his rookie season. At 18 he became the youngest player in the NHL. "The Kid" settled in comfortably in Vancouver. He had only one complaint about big-city life—there wasn't enough parking. He parked himself into a million-dollar home in the affluent British Properties of West Vancouver, but it didn't cost him a cent. He was a guest of Joanne and Harry Robinson. Their son, Brett, was away working in St. Louis. Joanne

LINDEN

Robinson was the former Joanne Hull, mother of Brett the hockey superstar and Bart the up-and-coming football player. Joanne, who was used to dealing with hockey players, said "Trevor had so much character for a boy his age. Someday he'll be a leader in the community as well as the team."

His first NHL coach, Bob McCammon, concurred: "He may never be a hundred-point man because he's too concerned about play in his own end of the ice. He's not going to win any scoring race but he is the kind of guy you need to win Stanley Cups."

Midway through his rookie year, the natural right winger had to shift to centre when the Canucks got hit by a plague of injuries. He wasn't a natural playmaker but his size and skating helped compensate. He was named the first star after his first game at centre, scoring one goal and setting up another. Instead of slowing down he picked up momentum and made a late drive for Rookie of the Year. He set a Canuck rookie scoring record with 30 goals. The Canucks paid for a promotional video to push his campaign for Rookie of the Year, but it still wasn't enough. A little eastern bias and an NHL-record 23 goals for a rookie defenseman won the award for the New York Ranger's Brian Leetch.

Linden was disappointed, but hardly heartbroken. He was second in Calder Cup voting, was named to the NHL All-Rookie team, and became the first Canuck rookie to win Team MVP. The newspaper devoted to hockey fanatics, *The Hockey News*, proved not everyone in the east is biased against the west by naming Linden their Rookie of the Year.

During the 1988–'89 playoffs, the Canucks came within one unlucky bounce of the puck in overtime in the seventh game to upsetting the eventual Stanley Cup winners, the Calgary Flames. The rookie scored three goals and had four assists. One of his goals was a memorable short-handed effort. He broke in alone on Theoren Fleury who was playing the point on the power play, and swept around the Calgary player like a man skating around a child. He ignored Fleury's desperate hooking and holding and swept in on Mike Vernon to score a goal that helped the Canucks force that seventh game scare. He amazed his older team-

mates like the veteran Harold Snepts, **LINDEN** pensate, he tried to do all the work using
who shook his head and remarked, "He's his size to muscle his away around the
one of the few young guys who's got his head offensive zone. It had worked on Fleury but it
squarely on his shoulders and isn't swept away by wasn't as successful against bigger, tougher defense-
all the glamour. He's another Stan Smyl, with more men. Mired in a slump, Linden was finally moved
natural scoring ability." back to the wing and responded with a late-season
surge that made his final stats respectable. He

His second season was like dropping the gloves wound up with 21 goals, down nine from his rookie
with Bob Probert, a painful experience that should year. Even more painful than the stat sheet was the
be forgotten as quickly as possible. His success as final standings—the Canucks finished fifth in the
centre the year before got him in the bad habit Smythe and missed the playoffs.
many young players fall into. He carried the puck Linden solved the sophomore slump the way he
too much. Not playing centre in junior, he'd never solved every other setback in his life—he worked
developed the natural passing ability of pure cen- harder. He spent the summer getting in the best
tres like Craig Janney and Adam Oates. To com-

shape of his life. The Canucks gave him **LINDEN** better than ever things to come in a mental lift by naming him one of three 1991–'92. Linden spent part of the off-co-captains. Pat Quinn had labelled Linden the season building a summer home in Whitefish, Canuck's captain for the next decade but he didn't Montana and getting in shape for the Canada Cup. want to put any undue pressure on the 20 year old He didn't make the team but the experience so he eased him into the role. Linden responded helped him get an early start on the season to during the 1990–'91 campaign with the best season come. Linden and the Canucks won on opening of his career. His 33 goals, 37 assists, 70 points night to move into first place in their division and helped carry the Canucks back into the playoffs. stayed there for the next 79 games. The supersti-That year he played in the All-Star game for the tious Linden spent the entire season driving exact-first time. As usual, he was the youngest player on ly the same route to the Pacific Coliseum.
the ice.

His superstition and leadership helped bring The Canucks were eliminated by Calgary in six respectability to a team that had set a record for games in the opening round of the playoffs; Linden mediocrity, having finished under .500 for 15 sea-had seven points in six games. He immediately sons in a row. At 21, Linden became the youngest joined Team Canada for the World Championships captain in the league (he shared the duties with and played well enough to win an invitation to the Vancouver defenseman Doug Lidster), and he was Team Canada training camp that summer for the among the scoring leaders for the first half of the Canada Cup.
season. He finally finished with a career and team-

The building blocks had been established for high 75 points.

More important and satisfying for Linden was the success of his team. The **LINDEN** Canucks set team records for wins, 42, and points, 96, and they won their division by 12 points. Their momentum was broken, however, by the late-season strike. In the first round of the playoffs, they almost got upset by the Winnipeg Jets, a team that had been almost unbeatable in the final month of the regular season. But Linden's pride helped the Canucks do what few teams had done before— bounce back after being down three games to one in the playoffs.

The comeback, however, took too much energy. Vancouver had nothing left for the fast and well-rested Edmonton Oilers. They eliminated the Canucks in six games. A depressed Trevor Linden sat forlornly in the new home he'd bought with his new contract that had made him the richest player in Canuck history. The beach was only a block away on a glorious late-spring morning, but Linden would not go out all day. "I'm getting a little better at handling losses," he said. "But it still hurts and leaves an empty feeling in your gut. Another goal or two and we'd still be playing. You always feel maybe you could have done more."

The warrior is never satisfied. He never stops working until the final victory is his. ★

Eric Lindros

It was a devastating body-check. A thundering fraction of a second that declared loudly that Eric Lindros had arrived. Yes, he could live up to the biggest hype since Gretzky. Yes, he was a boy who could play with men. And worst of all for the Quebec Nordiques, yes, he was worth millions.

LINDROS

LINDROS

For years the Swedish assassin Ulf Samuelsson had been terrorizing NHL forwards with his sneak attacks, destroying knees and careers. For years the NHL's designated red-neck Don Cherry had been foaming at the mouth on television as he replayed Samuelsson's kneeing and spearing, warning that "someday, somebody was going to get that guy and get him good."

That guy and that day finally arrived in September, 1991 in the Canada Cup. Canada versus Sweden. Samuelsson saw the avenger coming. It's hard to miss someone 6' 5" and 225 pounds, but he couldn't avoid him. Eric Lindros gathered up his massive bulk and fulfilled the fantasy of every NHL forward. He hurled himself at Samuelsson, driving him into the boards and protective glass. Samuelsson collapsed in a heap. Lindros skated away. Other players on the ice and bench joked that they felt like stopping the game and giving Lindros a standing ovation.

Samuelsson painfully skated away, holding his injured shoulder. He would not return to the series. Lindros and the Canadians went on to win easily in a tournament that did more than anything to convince the hockey world that Eric Lindros, boy legend, was not a mythical superhero created by the overactive imagination of sportswriters. He was the real thing.

The legend was born in London, Ontario in 1973, the son of athletic parents. His father Carl was a football player, good enough to be drafted by the Edmonton Eskimos of the Canadian Football League. He was also a good enough hockey player to play in the Chicago Blackhawks farm system. His mother Bonnie was a track and field star. Eric got his size from his dad, his drive and tenacity from his mom.

"I have a very strong sense of fairness and a strong sense of right and wrong" she boasted in a *Sports Illustrated* article about athletic stage mothers entitled 'Tough Moms'. "I learned it in a one-room country schoolhouse," she explained. "If something happened to you, someone tried to take advantage of you, your siblings came rushing to your rescue." NHL general managers take note. If you want to deal with Eric you have to deal with his mom. She's been there trying to remove real and imagined hurdles for Eric at every step of his hockey life.

Not that he ever seemed to need much help. He was a natural, dominating at every level of minor hockey and so in love with the game that when he was a youngster he refused to take off his hockey gear when he left the rink. Like most success stories, he knew early in Chapter One how the plot would unfold.

At twelve a school music teacher chided him for missing an important practise for a festival because he wanted to go to the world famous Pee Wee tournament in Quebec City. The teacher suggested that he get his priorities straight. The boy looked at the teacher in disbelief and said quietly, without being rude, that he did have his priorities in order; he was going to be a hockey player, not a musician.

Lindros, who had an enormous appetite (he'd eat five sandwiches for lunch plus have a loaf of raisin bread for a snack), quickly grew to his enormous size. At 13 he was playing against 16 year olds in Toronto's most famous hockey system, St. Mike's. Coach Scott MacLellan marvelled, "I couldn't blast him for mistakes like older players and he never sulked and was never intimidated. He was totally focussed on hockey."

To the rest of the world he was a boy wonder. To Carl and Bonnie Lindros he was still a boy. Their protectiveness would turn Lindros into the most controversial prodigy in the history of Canadian sport. It started when he was drafted by Sault Ste. Marie of the Ontario Junior Hockey League even though the family had warned them he would only be allowed to play in the Toronto area.

The Lindros reputation was born just after the draft when a furious Bonnie grabbed her 16-year-old son and hauled him away during an interview, telling the reporter to get lost and taking her son home. Instead of reporting to Sault Ste. Marie, they sent him to Detroit to play for a powerhouse midget team in a league that had sent Pat LaFontaine and Mike Modano to the NHL.

Eric spent the winter playing there before the OHL finally relented and invoked the Lindros rule, changing bylaws to let Sault Ste. Marie trade its first draft choice to Oshawa for six players and $80,000, an unprecedented price for one junior player. Lindros repaid Oshawa with huge dividends. Every game in Oshawa was sold out that spring as Eric—the "Next Great One"—carried the Generals to the 1990 Memorial Cup.

The next year he played on his second straight World Junior Championship team and led the OHL in scoring with 71 goals and 149 points in only 57 games. But with jeers of "Mommy's Boy" ringing in his ears, Lindros and the Generals were eliminated from the playoffs in the city he'd snubbed, Sault Ste. Marie.

What would a year be without a little controversy? In a near-instant replay of the great battle of the Soo, Lindros was drafted number one by Quebec even though his mom had again warned the Nordiques he'd never play for them. They'd forced the OHL to make him a special case and now Team Lindros was ready to take on the NHL. Eric insisted it was his decision and his stand: "My family, my friends, they know when I set my mind to something I don't back down." It was the stubbornness he'd inherited from his mother. She said, "I don't know why we're being criticized. We just want what's best for our son. Isn't that fair? Isn't that what any parent would do?"

Rightly or wrongly, Eric Lindros at 18 became a symbol of Canadian disunity. Disgruntled francophones saw more than economics and coincidence in a kid from Ontario refusing to play for a team in Quebec. But Lindros insisted everything was being overblown: "I don't think I represent Canada or the conflict in Canada. I think I represent player management relations in some companies, that's all."

As far as he was concerned, it was pure business. He'd play in Montreal but not in a tiny market like Quebec City where his off-ice income would be minimal. But the Nordiques took his continual snubs as merely posturing, just a part of the bargaining process, and they repeatedly turned down increasingly attractive offers from other teams for Eric "The Ingrate." There was even talk of Lindros challenging the NHL draft in court, a rumour that sent shudders through the shaky world of pro sports. But Lindros' lawyer insisted this was pure rumour, without foundation in fact.

While the controversy raged on, Lindros played on. He made believers of everyone and gained the respect of all he played with and against by becoming the youngest player ever invited to a Team Canada training camp, the youngest to ever make the team, and the youngest to help Canada win the Canada Cup. He spent the winter with the Canadian Olympic team and joined kids his own age for

LINDROS

another World Junior Championship.

It was a forgettable experience. He was ordinary; the rest of the team even worse. In key games and key situations, he made superb passes, the most underestimated and underpublicized part of his game. But his teammates couldn't finish off the plays and Canada had its worst junior tournament since the humiliation of the brawl in Prague in 1988.

Lindros salvaged his reputation in the Olympics. The phenom was a star attraction in Albertville. Everywhere he went he was followed by an entourage of fans and media—one group looking for autographs, the other group listening for quotes. "I think my role in life is to sell newspapers," he joked. There was no question he'd created more headlines than any 18 year old in Canadian history. His role in Albertville was to lead Canada to within a game of its first gold medal in 40 years at the Olympics. He was a star and one of the leading scorers of a team that did everything except win the final game, losing to what may be the last of the great teams from Russia.

Even that didn't stop the controversy. Critics pointed out if he was truly "The Next Great" he'd have been good enough to take control of that championship game all by himself and lift Canada to Olympic gold. Lindros was good, but he was no saviour. In that battle for the gold he was a war-weary foot soldier. He returned home exhausted, returned briefly to his junior team, then created more headlines and sold more newspapers by announcing his retirement for the year. At 18, Eric Lindros was a burn-out case.

At 18, the biggest thing most of us have accomplished is to finally clean up our own rooms. It's a bonus if we've become mature enough to also pick up our own socks. At 18, Eric Lindros had already been named player of the year in every league he ever played in, won the Canada Cup, won an Olympic silver medal, published his own autobiography, been the first choice in the NHL draft and become the centre of a cultural storm. Quebec hated him because he'd turned his back on a city and a culture. The rest of the country despised him as a greedy symbol of the modern spoiled athlete. The great Canadian hero had become the great Canadian villain.

"I don't think many people have made me out as

a villain," Lindros said in his own **LINDROS** Howe. "Eric Lindros has been proving defense, suggesting that if they had himself since he was six years old. they were exaggerating a problem that was simple These kids serve a thirteen-year apprenticeship; economics: "I just have my preferences about who even doctors don't do that."

I'd like to work for and I don't want to work for The apprenticeship of Eric Lindros is complete. Marcel Aubut (the Nordiques General Manager) Now he just wants to play. Anywhere. Anywhere and that's that." except Quebec City. "I'm hopeful I get traded," he

A superstar who truly was the great Canadian said. "I don't care where. I'll go anywhere, any- hero, Gordie Howe, felt the youngster had a case where with one exception." and shouldn't be vilified. "Eric Lindros is in the Well, it took some doing, but after 15 months he middle of all of it and if he ever decides to talk finally convinced the Quebec Nordiques that he about everything that's gone on it'll be a great was really serious about not playing there. And story," said Howe. The legend's face is scarred by when Marcel Aubut of the Nordiques finally got the 500 stitches he picked up during his long the message, he traded Lindros—not once but career. He still has aches and pains from the five twice. For the second year in a row all that anyone operations he went through and still has night- talked about at the NHL annual draft was Eric Lin- mares about the head injury that nearly ended his dros. The year before, Quebec was the only team life and his career before it even began. When he with a chance to acquire the superstar. This time was Lindros' age, Gordie Howe also held out for an he was everyone's for the bidding. outrageous signing bonus. Detroit finally relented The Lindros auction began with Philadelpia and gave him what he wanted: a team jacket. At putting in an opening bid of 15 million dollars and the peak of his career he never made more than half a dozen players. Aubut hastily accepted the $30,000 a season. He has a right to feel bitter and offer. Then he accepted an even better offer from fire charges of greedy at the new hockey kids on the New York Rangers who were willing to pay 25 the block, but he doesn't. million dollars.

"They deserve everything they can get," says Once again Eric Lindros had made history. He became the first player traded for a team to be named later! It took an NHL arbitrator eight days to sort through the mess. The Rangers had a signed deal with Quebec but Philadelphia had something even more binding in the old boy's world of business in the NHL—a handshake. They had their man-child. The arbitrator ruled the Flyers had that handshake an hour before the Rangers worked out their signed deal with Quebec. Lindros belonged to Philadelphia. The Rangers reluctantly agreed.

"I'm just happy to get out of there," said a relieved Lindros. "I didn't want any part of it. It lacked a winning spirit." He was thrilled to be heading to a team with a winning tradition. Wearing a Philadelphia cap Lindros told a news conference he hoped to be a Flyer for the next 15 years.

Was any 19 year old worth 15 million dollars and half a dozen players? The price Philadelphia paid was exhorbitant, but General Manager Russ Farwell didn't have any regrets. "You don't get a chance to trade for this kind of player very often," he said. "They come along only once in ten years. Bobby Clarke, who'd returned to the Philadelphia

LINDROS

front office after a short stay in Minnesota, agreed. "Lindros is not another Gretzky or Lemieux," he said. "He's unique. At 18 he proved he could play with the best in the world and he's only going to get better."

His coach in the Olympics, Dave King, had mixed feelings about the end of the Lindros affair. As Eric's old coach he was pleased but as Calgary's new coach he was concerned about facing a player he felt had no weaknesses. "He can stickhandle, he can pass, he can shoot and he's a physical force on the ice," says King. "Some players can only help you if they score a goal. I think Eric can go out there and change a game around with his body."

The teenage terror had already changed the game off the ice, now it was time for the Eric Lindros affair to end and the Eric Lindros era to begin in the NHL. After watching Lindros for years, New Jersey scout Marshall Johnston shook his head in mock pity for Lindros. "It's absolutely impossible for this guy to live up to everything that's been written about him," he says. "But even if he lives up to half of it, he's still going to be in the top ten percent of the game." ★

Mike Modano

You don't have to be a numerologist to understand the importance of the number nine. You only have to be a hockey fan. It's a number that signifies everything that is great about the game, even the great expectations. It's the NHL's most revered figure. Reserved for the extraordinary. Gordie Howe. Maurice Richard. Bobby Hull. And, of course, the player so great he wore not one but two nines at the same time, Wayne Gretzky. The teams that haven't already retired the number nine save it until someone very special and gifted comes along. Someone great enough to carry on the tradition of the number nine and mature enough to carry the pressure of wearing a number that can turn into a bulls-eye on your back.

On January 5, 1989 the Minnesota North Stars had the number nine waiting for their designated superstar when he stepped off the owner's private jet after a flight from Alaska where he'd starred for the U.S. in the World Junior Championships. Mike Modano spent the next 48 hours in a whirlwind of attention normally reserved for movie stars or rock and rollers. Everywhere he went he was interviewed, besieged by autograph hunters and fans who wanted him to assure them he could live up to his advance billing.

MODANO

Minnesota had waited a lot longer than it expected for the arrival of the **MODANO** baby-faced saviour. The kid—expected to turn on a city with his exciting end-to-end rushes, put life into a floundering franchise, and fill a near-empty building—had actually increased the public's disenchantment with the North Stars by holding them up for a king's ransom. The North Stars had passed up the old-fashioned, hard-working, dedicated hockey star—Trevor Linden—and had used the first pick in the 1988 draft to take Modano. Central Scouting had Modano and Linden rated as near equals. The scouts liked Modano's superior stickhandling and passing skills. There was no question he'd be a bigger scorer. But they also loved Linden's heart and attitude. There was no question that he'd be the bigger leader.

The North Stars were well aware that Linden could be a star but they felt Modano could be a superstar. Unfortunately for the North Stars, Modano's agent also knew how good and valuable his client could be. Howard Gourlitz, a tough negotiator from Modano's native Detroit, felt he was worth a lot more than Minnesota had offered.

When two months of talks failed to break the logjam he advised Modano to go home the day before training camp opened in September, 1988.

Modano spent the next three weeks at his parents home in Detroit where he'd once been a superstar with the powerhouse Detroit Caesars midget team.

When it was obvious the North Stars wouldn't budge he flew back to Prince Albert, Saskatchewan for another year with the Raiders of the Western Hockey League. He'd already scored 70 goals and nearly 200 points as a sixteen and seventeen year old. Minnesota was secretly pleased, as they felt Modano needed another year of junior anyway. "Deep inside, I didn't know if I was ready either," admitted Modano. "My only worry was how the players and fans would feel about the holdout when I finally did get to Minnesota."

He didn't have to worry. By mid-season a deal had finally been hammered out. After playing for the U.S. in the World Junior Championships in Alaska, Modano was flown to Minnesota on owner Gordon Gund's private jet. Thus began that famous whirlwind weekend that ended with Modano's debut in an exhibition game against a Soviet team. Modano didn't score. As a matter of fact he accidentally turned out to be the goat with a bad pass that gave the Soviets the winning goal. But the six-foot three-inch 18 year old wowed the fans and management with his speed **MODANO** ond to Calgary's rookie—in name and cleverness with the puck. Pierre only—Sergei Makarov. The veteran of Page, who was coaching the North Stars at the nearly a dozen Soviet national teams won the time, told reporters after the game, "He was every-Calder Trophy as NHL Rookie of the Year. *The* thing everyone told me he was. He's big. He's got *Hockey News* didn't regard Makarov as a real rookie good hands. He can pass the puck. He's got a good and named Modano Rookie of the Year. General shot. He just needs to work on his intensity and Manager Jack Ferreira, just before departing for the defensive play. I hate to say it because the kid's expansion San Jose Sharks, said "The thing about only 18 years old but he reminds me a lot of Jean Mike is that he's barely scratched the surface of Beliveau." what he can accomplish. It's scary to think what

After his wild weekend, Modano returned once he's going to do in this league."
again to Prince Albert. His accomplishments in When Ferreira moved out of the Minnesota junior hockey were starting to equal those of the front office, the legendary Bobby Clarke moved in Montreal legend. He was on his way to winning and was a little more reserved in his praise. "Mike the WHL scoring title when he broke his wrist in was an unbelievable junior," said Clarke. "He's still the All Star game. In just 41 games he'd scored 39 learning that in the NHL he has to apply himself goals and 105 points. The wrist healed in time for to play well. Lately he's finally started doing it."
him to join Minnesota in the '89 playoffs. While Clarke and new coach Bob Gainey brought a he didn't score, he got valuable Stanley Cup expe-new work ethic to Minnesota. They shifted rience that would help the North Stars in the Modano from centre to right wing where his defen-future. sive responsibilities would be lighter. It helped him

His first full season in the NHL proved Modano relax and find the missing flair that had caused a was worth the wait and the number nine. The bit-sophomore slump. Gainey said, "I don't know if I terness of his holdout was behind him. The team-expect more from Modano than he's putting on the mates he was worried about alienating welcomed scoreboard, but I do expect more from someone his him without reservations. Neil Broten was particu-size in the way of participation. I don't think he larly impressed by his hockey sense, "He's got a has to judge his impact in goals and assists. He can great head for the game. He doesn't get overconfi-do a lot of other things that give this team a lift."
dent or rattled." Modano responded with a late-season rush, scor-

Modano's only worry was getting enough ice ing in 12 of his last 14 games to finish with 64 time. In junior he had a free hand to do what he points, down 11 from his rookie year. But he wanted and play when he wanted. Power plays. redeemed himself with 20 points in 23 games in Killing penalties. He logged 30 to 40 minutes a the Miracle of Minnesota. The North Stars, the game. Suddenly, in Minnesota, he was down to last team to sneak into the playoffs, were the last sometimes only three or four minutes a game. He team eliminated, making it all the way to the finals scored his first goal in his first regular season game before surrendering the Stanley Cup to Pittsburgh.
with his parents proudly watching from the stands. During the 1991–'92 season, Modano and the But Page, a stern, defensive disciplinarian, kept the North Stars couldn't regain the momentum of that kid on the bench for much of the game and much incredible run to the Stanley Cup finals. The team of the first half of the season. He constantly harped slipped back to its old level of mediocrity, while about Modano's backchecking and concentration. Modano continued to search for that break-out "It was tough not to play," recalls Modano. "There season that would lift him from good to great. He were a lot of ups and downs and a lot to learn. It had career highs of 33 goals and 44 assists to lead took a couple of months to get used to it and feel at the North Stars in scoring for the first time.
home." Number 9 is still trying to live up to the promise

Offensively, he could still do it all, even in the Jack Ferreira, his old general manager, said in his NHL. Not all the cute little moves he got away rookie year, "Mike's a natural, and he's having fun. with in junior worked in the NHL, but enough did Once he concentrates for 60 minutes, 80 games a that he scored 29 goals and 75 points to finish sec-year, we're all going to have fun. Watching." ★

Alexander Mogilny

February 18, 1992 The Unified team from what was once the Soviet Union was preparing to play Finland in the opening game of the medal round of the Olympics.

The right winger who was supposed to help ensure the continued domination of the Russians wasn't in the Unified lineup. Alexander Mogilny wasn't even in Albertville, France. He was in Vancouver in the middle of his third season with the Buffalo Sabres, peeling off a soggy uniform after a high-paced practise for a game the next night with the Canucks.

MOGILNY

MOGILNY

It was Mogilny's 23rd birthday. His face, normally as dour and lifeless as the cities in his native country, came alive in a bright smile when his teammates suddenly surrounded him singing "Happy Birthday." He should have known better when the team comedian, goalie Clint Malarchuk, handed him a birthday cake. Mogilny bent forward and suddenly realized his mistake. Before he could move Marlarchuk shoved the cake, actually made of shaving cream, into Mogilny's face. Mogilny laughed as loud as everyone else after falling for the oldest trick in the practical joker's book. It was a lighthearted moment that showed how far Alexander Mogilny had come in three years.

In May of 1989, three days after helping the Soviets win another World Championship, Alexander Mogilny made an historic flight to freedom. The Russian rebel, tired of living under the iron fist of Soviet Coach Viktor Tikhonov, became the first Russian hockey player to defect.

It was a journey that actually began twenty years earlier in the city of Khabarovsk, thousands of miles east of Moscow, near the Siberian border. Alexander was the youngest of two sons born to Geddady and Nadezha Mogilny. In a city where winter lasted for eight months it was inevitable that little Alexander would learn to skate almost as soon as he learned to walk. By the age of six he was already hearing people marvel at his great skating ability. The smooth, powerful strides that would someday carry him to the NHL came naturally to him.

He played soccer in the summer but hockey quickly became his great love. Any kind of hockey. There wasn't an indoor rink in his hometown, so he spent the winter learning to skate through the snow, leaning into a heavy Siberian wind—20 to 30 degrees below zero. It didn't matter. Fifteen years later Alexander's eyes still come alive as he remembers the sheer joy of those long childhood hours on that frozen rink—sweet memories shared by generations of Canadian kids.

"It's fun. You don't even feel the cold," recalls Alexander. "You don't even realize how cold it is outside because you're so into the game. Your nose turns white. You can't feel your cheeks or your fingers, but you don't care. You just play hockey. You come home—everythings hurts. But you have so much fun you don't care. It's great. Everybody's gotta go through this kind of stuff."

Those pickup games on an outdoor rink helped him develop the skating and stickhandling skills that would make Mogilny a star in the Soviet Union. He was ten before he decided it was time to get serious about the game. "I realized it would be my bread and butter," he says. He didn't think about anything except hockey. His goal was not the NHL. He'd never even heard about that. His goal wasn't even to make the national team in distant Moscow, an eight-hour flight away. His goal was to make his hometown team which played in the Russian equivalent of the minor leagues.

Mogilny made it when he was only 14. "In my first game, I score my first goal on almost my first shift and I think 'Oh God, I made it!' It was a great experience." The scouts quickly flocked to this far eastern city to see this kid who could outskate men. He got an invitation to try out for the Red Army team, and at 15 he was absolutely thrilled with how far hockey had taken him. He practised with the junior Red Army club and worked his way up to the number one team two years later.

He'd surpassed even his wildest dreams but the reality was slowly turning into a nightmare under the dictatorial Viktor Tikhonov. Hockey was the easy part. He broke into the Red Army starting lineup at 17 and scored 15 goals in 28 games. In 1998, Mogilny became the youngest Soviet hockey star to ever play in the Olympics. The kid from Khabarovsk celebrated his 18th birthday in Calgary, scoring three goals and setting up two others on the way to the Olympic gold medal. That came just a month after he'd been named the top forward at the 1988 World Junior Championships. His career had never been better, but his life had never been worse.

"I was so young and the coaches were so old. They did not know how to relate to younger people. They did everything for me, even my thinking. I did not have a life. I didn't have any free time to see my friends or have a social life. I looked at the older players—Larionov, Makarov, Fetisov—and I said this is not for me. I see how this guy is treating our stars and I say it cannot go like that for me because my career is just starting." His performance started to reflect the misery and dreariness of his life off the ice. His goal-scoring totals declined every year with the Red Army team. Upset with Mogilny's listless performance in one game at the Olympics, the unrelenting Tikhonov physically hit Mogilny to wake him up.

That was literally the final blow for him. The hatred for Tikhonov was the driving force. Seeing his old teammates Larionov, Fetisov and Makarov move to the NHL was the inspiration for his own plan for freedom. After helping the Soviets win the 1989 World Championships in Stockholm, Mogilny met with Gerry Meehan, general manager of the Buffalo Sabres. The Sabres had drafted him in the fifth round the year before. Details of the defection are still secret but within a few hours Mogilny was on his way to New York.

The Sabres did everything they could to make the transition as painless as possible but it was still the most difficult year of his life. His mother burst into tears when he phoned home to tell her he defected. The KGB wiretapped the Mogilny home and cut off the call before he could convince his mother he'd made the right decision. To top it all off, his English was as bad as your average NHLer's understanding of Russian. He did get some help from a Soviet friend who'd earlier defected to Sweden, and then travelled with Mogilny to New York.

Mogilny had been a junior lieutenant in the Red Army, a technicality required of all hockey players on the Red Army team. To the NHL he was a defector. To the Soviets he was a deserter, a traitor. They wanted him back. The tension and anxiety transferred into a strange new symptom that threatened his new career in the NHL—he became terrified of flying. Midway through his first season he was reduced to playing at home or in games on the eastern seaboard that he could get to by car or bus. It took months of therapy and professional help to finally cure him. "I never had

MOGILNY

this fear of flying before. Something just changed inside me because of all I'd gone through: the frustration of playing for Tikhonov, the change in atmosphere. Things around me changed so completely," he says. "My doctor said it's natural for me to have problems. But now I feel great. I have no more problems."

Convinced that it was a manifestation of his anxieties, Mogilny relaxed and the problems disappeared. On the ice he always felt comfortable, despite the smaller ice surface, the strange style of play where players seemed more intent on hitting than scoring, and a language that kept him from understanding his coaches or talking to his team-

mates. He scored 15 goals and had 28 assists in 65 games in his troubled rookie season.

His second year began as another season of frustration. Coach Rick Dudley certainly wasn't another Tikhonov but he was starting to wonder if it was time to get tough with the shy, moody Mogilny who was by now being nicknamed "the Russian Riddle." The talent was obvious. Teammate Phil Housley, one of the best skaters in the NHL, marvelled at Mogilny's effortless skating. "He has great lateral movement and breakaway speed," noted Housley. "His hands and feet are quick. He's going to be an impact player."

But when? That's what the Sabres and their fans were starting to wonder. Injuries slowed the start of his second season, and he missed 18 games. The layoff gave him more time to adjust to his new life and new land. Television is a great teacher of language, and the vast wasteland of daytime television helped Mogilny improve his English. His teammates watched him slowly come out of his shell.

John Muckler, who'd come over from the Edmonton Oilers to help Meehan in the Buffalo front office, said, "Alex is a very intelligent, shy guy. Very comfortable being by himself. He hasn't learned to be comfortable around the public. People read him the wrong way. He's getting along great with his teammates. He's got a dry sense of humour. I think he's great."

Recovered from his injuries, Mogilny finally became the star that the Sabres had gone through all the trouble for. In his last 31 games he scored 22 goals and wound up with a 30-goal season. His individual brilliance and success, however, didn't satisfy him. Long years in the Soviet team system had conditioned him to forget about his own performance: the only true measurement is team success. Tikhonov had branded Mogilny

MOGILNY

as selfish, and predicted he'd be out of hockey within two years of his defection. Ironically, his old coach would be proud to learn how unselfish Mogilny had become.

"My first year was tough," says Mogilny, "second year wasn't that bad. I went through a tough period and now I look back and laugh at myself." He'd proven he belonged, yet he still wasn't happy. "I don't think it's right to worry about your own stats. Fifty, sixty goals don't mean a thing if the team doesn't win. We haven't made it past the first round of the playoffs. We gotta do better than that," he says.

The Sabres couldn't have agreed more. Early in

the 1991–'92 season, Mogilny's third, they fired Rick Dudley and talked Muckler into taking over the team. They also traded the next Gilbert Perrault, Pierre Turgeon, to the Islanders for Pat LaFontaine. Muckler put the fun and the speed back into the Sabres game. The quick pace of practises and emphasis on skating reminded Mogilny of the Red Army workouts. In LaFontaine he found a centre who was almost as fast as his linemate back home—Pavel Bure. He also found another fan. LaFontaine was amazed. "I played with a lot of great players with the Islanders and Alex has to be the most talented I've ever seen," says LaFontaine. "He's got five different gears. He's a great puck-handler. He's just going to get better and better."

In his third year, Mogilny improved in every offensive category, posting his second straight 30-goal season. More importantly, he became part of the team. He was not the self-centred pouter that Tikhonov had predicted. He'd also discovered a new love, golf. He became consumed by the most capitalist of games, and in one year went from being a total beginner to having a 16 handicap. Life was never better for the kid who hadn't known summer or vacations back home where life consisted of 11 months of hockey and life in an army barracks.

"It's beautiful here. There's so much freedom," he says with awe. "I play golf all summer. I like to travel and see the country and play golf in these places."

Alexander Mogilny has come a long way in only three years, and the journey is just beginning.   ★

Owen Nolan

This is the era of the quick fix. "We want everything and we want it now" has become the rallying cry of the 90s. The world's most famous and successful restaurant is a fast-food drive-in. Pizza companies promise you your money back if they don't deliver within half-an-hour. Companies are competing to produce simpler and faster microwaves. The remote control has become the most popular form of exercise—if we don't like what we're watching we change it instantly. We've got instant on, instant off, instant cash, instant credit and, unfortunately for the new breed of athlete, we demand instant success.

NOLAN

No one is more painfully aware of that than Owen Nolan of the Quebec Nordiques. He was nearly crushed under the burden of being the first player drafted by the NHL in the '90s. Quebec took him number one in 1990 even though they were aware that two or three other players—including Jaromir Jagr and Mike Ricci—were further advanced and closer to being ready to step quickly and easily from junior hockey to the NHL. Jagr had better hands and trickier moves. Ricci had a more balanced game and emotional maturity. But Nolan had better size and toughness. He was what every team can never get enough of—a big, rugged winger who could beat

NOLAN

you with his hands or his body. It was part of his heritage.

Nolan was born in a city permanently on war alert: Belfast, Northern Ireland. "I left when I was seven months old and never really go back," he says brusquely, not eager to talk about something that would make him a little different. All he ever wanted to do was fit in and be one of the boys. His family settled in Thorold, Ontario, near Niagara Falls. When he was nine years old he wanted to be a goalie but somebody else beat him to the goalie pads. The coach of the team made a fateful decision, moving the solid-looking youngster to forward. Fans in Quebec would be amused to hear he was an instant success. His dad, Owen senior, chuckles that he couldn't skate very well but he was always a natural goal scorer: "He got a hat trick in his very first game as forward."

Nolan continued scoring as he moved up to bantam hockey. His skating was still questionable but Jim Cherry, head scout of the Cornwall Royals of the Ontario Hockey League, saw something that no one else did. Cornwall drafted him even though the Central Scouting Bureau had him ranked 251st. Coach Marc Crawford, a former NHLer with Vancouver, saw what Cherry had seen in Nolan, "A Cam Neely in the rough. He's tougher than nails. He's got great fists and he can score. If he can't go around someone he'll go through them."

Nolan became a man among boys in junior hockey. At 6' 1" and 195 pounds he owned the corners and could still score goals—34 in his rookie junior season along with 213 penalty minutes that stood as testimony to his toughness. He didn't back down against older kids. Even though scouts felt his play tailed off and he wasn't as physical as he should have been in his final year of junior, he still came up with a rare combination of 50 goals (51), 100 points

(110), and 200 minutes in penalties (240).

NOLAN

Quebec didn't hesitate for a second in making him the first player drafted in the 1990 Entry Draft. But a year later critics were using Nolan as an example of why Quebec was the worst team in the league. There was no instant success, only instant failure. Aware of all the doubts that he couldn't play the same bruising, bullish style in the NHL as he had in junior, Nolan decided to muscle-up in the summer before his rookie season.

It was a big mistake. A 207 pound mistake. That's how much he weighed after a summer of weightlifting. Twelve pounds heavier than in his junior days. "I thought it would help but it slowed me down. I'm a lot more effective at 195. As a junior I could overpower guys but in this league the guys are too tough to catch and too big to hit."

A slower Nolan could barely keep up with the helter skelter pace of the NHL. He lost confidence and played tentatively, almost timidly, afraid to take offensive chances and worried about making a defensive mistake. He was a shadow of the player the Nordiques thought they were getting. Wisely, they refused to panic.

"If you looked at his play at the end of his rookie season," explained coach Pierre Page, "you could see him coming on. If he'd played that way all year he'd have been as good as anyone." Within a year, he was. He'd finished a dismal rookie season with just three goals and 13 points, but eight of his points came in the last two weeks of the season. "I want to start next season the same way I ended this one," he said, "scoring points and being aggressive."

During the 1991–'92 season he was even better than he hoped. The instant success that people had wanted just took an extra year to arrive. When it did, Nolan was everything the Nordiques wanted and more. They expected a 30-goal man, they got 40. Twelve pounds lighter, he was a new and quicker man. His skating improved immensely. Surprisingly, with less muscle he seemed to be even stronger, and didn't fade in the third period of games.

Nolan scored 20 goals faster than anyone in the NHL, faster even than those scoring machines Hull and Lemieux. He played in his first all-star game. He tired and slumped in mid-season when his centre, Joe Sakic, was sidelined with injuries. But he rebounded late in the season when Page teamed him up with the talented Europeans, Mats Sundin and Valeri Kamensky. In one brilliant game, the line produced eight goals in a late season 10–4 victory in Hartford that ended Quebec's 38 game winless streak on the road. Nolan had a goal and set up 5 others. "The chemistry worked really well," said Nolan after a game that showed how far he'd come in his development as a complete NHL player.

Nolan finished the year with 42 goals, 73 points and a robust 181 minutes in penalties. The Nordiques expect him someday soon to duplicate his 50–100–200 performance in junior. The Nordiques' patience has been rewarded. Owen Nolan wants to prove that lasting success is better than instant success any day. ★

Mark Recchi

Height: 5 feet, 10 inches
Weight: 195 pounds

On paper, Mark Recchi doesn't look small. On the ice he doesn't play small. Yet somehow in the eyes of NHL scouts, Mark Recchi looked like Theoren Fleury's little brother.

Growing up in Kamloops, British Columbia Mark Recchi certainly didn't feel small. Heck, he was a giant in the Recchi household. The one everyone called when they needed something off the top shelf. His Dad, Mel, is 5' 5" tall, towering three inches above his mother, Ruth. Tall is a foreign word in the Recchi household. Mark, the second youngest, grew to be the tallest of them all.

When the Recchis leafed through the book of names for their sons, they got stuck on the pageful of M's. First came Mike, then Marty and Mark and finally Matt. The boys weren't tall but they were solid, leaning toward the stocky build their Dad had reached in middle age. They were also athletic. Mike the eldest loved speed, on water skis and motocross bikes. Marty was a football player, small but tough, preferring to run over things rather than around them. Mark and Matt, the youngest, were lured by the ice rink not far from their home.

RECCHI

89

Mark faced the same problem with every team he played for. He had to convince them he was big enough. When you're small and talented, you're an easy and obvious target for those who have the size but not the skill for the game. They tried to run Recchi out of every rink he played in. Most of the assassins who had him in their sights at every step of his career are now long gone. Recchi goes on, dodging the cheap-shot artists with deft feet, flashing hands and darting eyes that quickly find the open man.

Actually Recchi owes a debt to the scouts who thought he was too small and the goons who thought he was an "easy mark." When they took dead aim on Recchi, they left a lot of open ice behind them. Often they also left the man they were checking. With the courage of a kid who's used to being picked on and the quickness of a kid who has to find something to compensate for his size, Recchi would wait until the last possible second, and then zip a pass to the open man, duck under his checker and churn back into the play with short, choppy strides. Often it resulted in a 2 on 1 or a 3 on 2 that led to a great scoring chance. Thanks to the big guys, little Mark Recchi developed into the best passing winger in the league, every league he played in.

He was a high-scoring star at each level of minor hockey in Kamloops. Quick and clever. Not big, yet solid on his skates. He picked the right role model. His hero was another guy who was supposed to be too brittle for the rough stuff. Another guy who was a pretty fair passer, another guy with deceptive quickness and speed. A guy named Wayne Gretzky.

Supporting four robust sons can be expensive. Mel Recchi was part owner of the *Kamloops News*. It was a small, struggling newspaper, battling to hold its own against the big-city invaders, the *Vancouver Sun* and *Province*. The Recchis didn't have a lot of money but they had enough to support the kids increasingly active and expensive sports activities. Mark was already developing enough to hint that his dreams of an NHL career were not just fantasies.

A kid with Recchi's talent and proven scoring ability should have been a natural to step up to the big team in town. The Kamloops Blazers were establishing a dynasty in the Western Hockey

RECCHI

League. They looked at Recchi but again they were blinded by one statistic, his size. The little guy was heartbroken until he got a call from New Westminster. The big bad Bruins were no longer big or bad. Their reign of terror in junior hockey had ended with the graduation of monsters named Barry Beck and Harold Philipoff. They saw in Mark Recchi the second coming of Stan Smyl, a fireplug with heart and desire that wiped out any "short"comings.

They gave Recchi the chance he wanted and he made the most of it, getting 61 points for a very weak team. He continued a pattern that's followed him throughout his career, setting up more goals than he scores—a rarity for a winger. It reinforced his growing reputation as a creative passer. More importantly he proved he could survive in the insanely chippy world of junior hockey, where fights traditionally outnumber goals each night.

New Westminster was a floundering franchise on the verge of extinction. They were happy to trade their best young player, Mark Recchi, back to his hometown in return for a couple of other young prospects. The Bruins wanted bodies, not skill. The Blazers want to correct their mistake. They should never have let Recchi get out of town and they knew it.

Coach Ken Hitchcock was putting together a team that would dominate the west for the next four years with future NHLers like Recchi, Rob Brown, Greg Hawgood and Dave Chyzowski. Recchi was a big part (a pun fully intended) of Hitchcock's plans. Any doubts Hitchcock had disappeared when he met the family. "His brothers, his dad, his mom. They're all the same," he recalls. "There's a competitive instinct there, a burning desire. Recchi tradition is that you come to play." A cliche, but an apt one for Mark Recchi.

His first season in Kamloops, 1986–'87, he came out flying. He had 76 points when he broke his ankle 40 games into the season. It cost him the rest of the year and something even more important. He was completely ignored in his first year of eligibility for the NHL draft. Now, next to the too-small rating on the negative side of the scouting report the NHL scouts added another qualifier, too fragile. By now, Recchi was too conditioned to rejection to be heartbroken. "I was having a great year until I broke my ankle and that seemed to turn everybody off," he says. "But I knew I could play in the NHL so I just kept working."

RECCHI

And scoring 61 goals. A league-leading 93 assists. 154 points in 62 games in 1987–'88. He led Kamloops to the West Division Championship and he finally made the NHL think twice by playing a vital role in Canada's gold medal at the World Junior Championships in Moscow. Recchi was the key to a checking line that stopped the fastest skaters in the world—Sergei Fedorov and Alexander Mogilny.

Recchi had proven he could hold up to the nightly assaults in junior hockey. He'd proven he could score wherever he played. And he proved he was fast enough in his own awkward way to keep up with the fastest of the fleet. But the NHL wasn't as fast as the Kamloops Blazers to admit they had made a mistake. Every team in the league passed him over again, and again, and again. Finally, in the fourth round, Pittsburgh's western scout Bruce Haralson convinced the Penguins to take a chance on Recchi. Haralson had once been the chief scout in Kamloops. He'd made a mistake on Recchi once. He wasn't about to let it happen again. Looking back without bitterness, Recchi shrugs off the disappointment of being the 67th player taken in the 1988 draft. "I knew I wouldn't be an overnight sensation, but I felt that I had the tools and eventually my time would come."

His confidence and patience were rewarded. Eventually. His usual hard work in training camp earned him a spot in the opening lineup. But his career got off to a nervous start. After scoring only once in 15 games he was shipped down to the minors. The perserverance he developed in having to prove himself nearly every year he played hockey had finally paid off. He had to do it one more time, and did he ever. The rookie tore up the International Hockey League, scoring 50 goals and setting up 99 others for Muskegon.

Ironically, the great year was almost the worst thing that ever happened to him. The Penguins feared he was a minor league superstar who was too slow and too small to make it in the big leagues. Despite a training camp that was even better than his first, Recchi was back on the plane to Muskegon to start the 1989–'90 season. Again, a lot of players would have hung their heads and let

the rejection ruin their careers. Not Recchi. He was used to it. The year before he tore up the IHL. This time he destroyed it. Seven goals, four assists, eleven points in only four games. "The Little Recchi Ball" had finally convinced everyone.

Pittsburgh Coach Gene Ubriaco had made the decision to demote Recchi. He still wasn't convinced he was more than a marginal journeyman and didn't play Recchi that much. But by Christmas the unpopular Ubriaco was gone, fired and replaced by General Manager Craig Patrick. He united Recchi with John Cullen and Kevin Stevens and Recchi knew he'd finally made it. He made a late charge at Rookie of the Year, scoring 30 goals and assisting on 37. There's that more assists than goals ratio again. It was a performance worthy of praise and a raise, but he didn't get either. He finished a distant third to Sergei Makarov and Mike Modano in Rookie of the Year voting.

Recchi still had something to prove. **RECCHI** Pittsburgh and the equally-surprising He joined his linemates in a daring move. Minnesota North Stars tied at two games All three refused to sign new contracts, playing out the option year of their original deal. With the support of the fatherly new coach, Bob Johnson, the Option Line led the Penguins into the playoffs for the first time in years. Recchi scored 40 goals and set up 73. The best bargain in the league was the only player in the league to score more points than thousands of dollars. He gave Pittsburgh 113 points for the $105,000 they paid him that year. As a bonus he threw in an inspirational performance that took the Penguins to their first Stanley Cup victory.

It didn't surprise Paul Coffey, a teammate who'd played with a couple of pretty fair players in his days in Edmonton. He said, "The word that comes to mind when you mention Recchs is competitor. He's a great kid with a big heart. I mean he's 5' 8" or whatever the hell he is (5' 10") but he plays about 6' 5"—he's a big game player."

Recchi lived up to the praise. He produced big game after big game. The weight-lifting program that helped him add twenty pounds of muscle to his solid frame provided the endurance and stamina he needed to survive the marathon Stanley Cup playoffs. Survive was the operative word.

The eternally enthusiastic Badger Bob Johnson had done the seemingly impossible with the Penguins. He'd taken a team rich in offensive talent and given them just enough defense and discipline to win. The Penguins had a Cadillac named Lemieux, and a Ferrari named Coffey but it was a Jeep named Recchi that got them going when they got bogged down. Opposing teams quickly realized Recchi was the emotional heart of the team. He became a marked man. He was also their leading scorer until the bumps and bruises and the grind of playing more than 110 games finally caught up with him in the Stanley Cup finals.

"I picked an awful time to play poor hockey," he remembers, "but sometimes you just don't have the legs." Then, with his characteristic confidence he added "But I was sure I'd be able to contribute before it was over."

He couldn't have picked a better time. With apiece in the finals, Recchi finally found new life in his tired legs. One minute, that's all it took to decide the game and the series. Late in the first, Mario Lemieux fed Recchi a pass. He leaned his 190 pounds into the shaft of his stick. It bent and then boomeranged back, whipping the puck past a startled Jon Casey in the North Star's goal. Less than a minute later he was back to show a delighted sellout crowd in Pittsburgh how he got the nickname. The Recchi Ball got bounced off his feet but kept rolling and somehow managed to bang the puck by Casey. The two goals turned out to be the difference. Pittsburth went on to take the game and the Cup in six games.

"It was an unreal season," said Recchi in a burst of understatement. It was a season he'd dream about that summer back in Kamloops. A season that proved hard work is more than it's own reward. Recchi's gamble had paid off. The Penguins finally gave Recchi a new contract that would make him a very rich young man. The little guy who thought he could had finally chugged his way to the top of the mountain, and then he came tumbling down the other side.

The beloved coach Bob Johnson died of brain cancer. The moody, unpredictable and eternally disgruntled Scotty Bowman took over behind the bench. Recchi's production fell off and late in the season with the Penguins struggling to make the playoffs, Recchi became the centrepiece in a desparate five-player trade that brought the bigger and tougher Rick Tocchett to the Penguins.

No year would be complete without Recchi having to prove himself again, and succeeding again. Recchi was in tears when he learned he was leaving Pittsburgh but he quickly made himself right at home in his new home. He took Philadelphia by storm. He was reunited with his old junior coach, Ken Hitchcock, who had moved on to become assistant coach of the Flyers. Recchi got more ice time than ever and scored more than ever.

At long last, it looks like Mark Recchi has finally found a team that will really appreciate him. ★

Mike Ricci

There are players who are famous for making great plays. They're fan favorites. Then there are players who are famous for never making bad plays. They're coaches' favorites. Mike Ricci is one of those players who does everything a coach could want and occasionally even a little bit more. From the time he started playing hockey in his native Scarborough, Ontario, through his steady progress up the ladder to NHL success, Mike Ricci has always done the little things that win more admiration than applause.

He was always a leader, another coach on **RICCI** try. If he'd been eligible for the 1989 draft the ice. The son of parents from the large he'd have been the first or second choice, Italian community in the Toronto area, Ricci after scoring 54 goals and 106 points. But he had to inherited the hard-work ethic that makes so many wait another year before he was old enough to be immigrants such a success in their new country. His drafted.

idols weren't the flashy players who thrived on It was almost a wasted year. He injured his speed and daring, they were the quietly efficient shoulder and played hurt for most of the season. It superstars of effort like Gordie Howe and Bobby forced him to slow down his crashing, bashing Clarke. style. But he also got the thrill of his hockey life

Ricci's exceptional maturity and leadership were when the Canadian junior team, with him again quickly recognized and rewarded in junior hockey. serving as captain, won the 1990 World Junior At 17, and in his second season with Peterborough title. By the time the Ontario Hockey League play- Petes of the Ontario Hockey League, he was named offs started, however, Ricci was tired and worn their captain, as well as being named captain of the down. The previous year he'd averaged two points Canadian team at the World Junior Champi- a game in the playoffs. In the spring of 1990 he got onships. Ricci was the star of the Canadian team just 12 points in 12 games. and was easily the best junior prospect in the coun- He wouldn't admit it but he also appeared to be

affected by his decline in the ratings of **RICCI** junior prospects. He'd gone from a consensus number one before the season started to being ranked fourth behind Owen Nolan, Petr Nedved and OHL scoring champion Keith Primeau. It was hard for Ricci not to be demoralized even though he ended his junior career with a glittery array of awards. Canadian Junior Player of the Year. The OHL's Outstanding Player and Most Gentlemanly Player awards. The scouts explained that he didn't get any worse. The others simply got a lot better.

Everyone knew Ricci was the only one of the top four prospects who would definitely and easily slip into the starting lineup the next season. Quebec, Vancouver and Detroit drafted ahead of Philadelphia and decided to gamble on the potential of Nolan, Nedved and Primeau. The Flyers were happy to settle for the sure thing. They passed up another potential superstar, Jaromir Jagr, for Mike Ricci—the certain leader they hadn't had since Bobby Clarke retired.

The Flyers put him with the regulars in the team yearbook, something they hadn't done for a rookie in a decade. They also predicted his number 18 would someday earn a spot next to Clarke's famous number 16 in the rafters of the Philadelphia Spectrum. Another Flyer who'd never quite lived up to his billing as the next Clarke, Rick Tocchet, was impressed by Ricci at training camp. "I think he'll turn out to be the best player in the draft," said Tocchet. "He's out to prove he should have been number one. The fans are going to love him. He works hard at both ends of the ice." That last cliche is the highest praise a hockey star can give a young player. Coach Paul Holmgren agreed: "He's a big guy for us defensively as well as offensively. He's a well-rounded player."

The 18 year old insisted he wasn't out to prove any scouts were wrong. His actions on the ice told another story. He had a superb training camp. In his first NHL game in the pre-season, he showed how valuable he could become as he set up one goal and scored the tying one in a come-from-behind tie. Nothing in Peterborough had quite prepared him for the high of playing in front of the infamously rabid fans in Philadelphia.

"I just skated around wondering what I was doing there," he recalls. "It's loud. It's big. It's everything you dreamed of." Ricci was still in awe on opening night of the regular season in Boston a couple of weeks later. "It was like a dream, standing there during the national anthem with the crowd in the Garden going crazy."

A few minutes later that dream and his finger were broken. He shattered it trying to do the little things he'd always done by reflex, sacrificing his body to block a shot. His NHL career was on hold for a month. He missed 11 games. When he did return it was like starting all over again. "The defensemen in the NHL are so big," he said. "It's tough. There's so much hooking. I skate pretty straight up and when they hit me high I go down pretty easily." Despite the problems he still worked his way up to the Flyer's top line with Tocchet and Pelle Eklund. He became only the ninth Flyer rookie to score 20 goals, finishing with 21 goals and 20 assists. He wasn't NHL Rookie of the Year, but he did outscore all the players taken ahead of him in the draft.

Unlike the Nordiques, Canucks and Red Wings, the Flyers had no regrets, no second thoughts about the player they'd taken. The hard-working rookie rewarded himself with some well-deserved time off. Soccer was his second love. As a youngster growing up, he was a good enough player to have been a prospect for the Canadian national team. He traveled to Italy to visit relatives and watch the world's biggest team sporting spectacle—the World Cup of Soccer.

Ricci returned rested, revived and healthy for

the first time in two years. "I just want to help the team make the playoffs more than anything," he vowed before his sophomore season began. "There are a lot of new faces so you don't know what kind of atmosphere you're going to play in."

Before the 1991–'92 season was over, however, there'd be even more new faces. The Flyers were destined to finish dead last in the toughest division in hockey, the Patrick, even though they wound up with enough points to have finished as high as third in the Adams or fourth in the Norris. They changed coaches. They changed stars. They traded the once untouchable Tocchet to Pittsburgh for the smaller but higher scoring Mark Recchi. They got another of the rising stars of the NHL, Rod Brind'amour, from St. Louis. And they picked up Wes Walz from Boston.

"We're building something positive here now," said a relieved Ricci at the end of the year. "We're young. We've got some veterans who keep us stable. We've got a good mix. The young guys are looking to the future. We want to win." The six-footer scored 20 goals for his second straight season and with 56 points wound up fourth in team scoring behind Recchi, Brind'amour and the new coach's son, Kevin Dineen.

The Flyers finished last in the Patrick division

RICCI

but they had the second best defense in the division, giving up fewer goals than anyone except the team that finished on top of the entire 1991–'92 standings, the New York Rangers. The Flyers defensive total was a telling statistic that, coupled with the stockpiling of young talent, makes the Flyers a team to watch in the 90s.

Ricci's value to the Philadelphia Flyers was underlined in June, 1992 when he became one of the key figures in the trade of the decade. Philadelphia reluctantly sent Ricci, goaltender Ron Hextall, centre Peter Forsberg, defensemen Steve Duchesne and Kerry Huffman along with 15 million dollars to Quebec City for Eric Lindros. "The player we hated to give up the most was Mike Ricci," explained Philadelphia General Manager Russ Farwell. "We know he's going to be a solid player in this league for a very long time. But you have to give up quality to get quality and we couldn't pass up the chance to get a player like Lindros. The deal wouldn't have gone through if we hadn't included Ricci."

At first Ricci was heartbroken. He wanted to be a part of the rebuilding of the Flyers. "It's a difficult situation for everyone," admitted Ricci. "But you've got to deal with what's thrown at you. I just hope I can be happy here." ★

Jeremy Roenick

Know a man's heroes and you know the man. Jeremy Roenick grew up in Boston idolizing Terry O'Reilly and Ray Bourque. Not the naturally gifted superstars like Bobby Orr or Phil Esposito but super workers like Bourque and the ultimate Bruin, O'Reilly.

But Roenick's been labelled a throwback since the day he broke into the NHL. In the feature profile of its pre-season hockey edition in the fall of 1991, *Sports Illustrated* used bold two-inch headlines to officially declare Jeremy Roenick "A Blast From The Past."

Open a time capsule from the NHL of the '40s and '50s and Jeremy Roenick could pop out. He's been called the Second Coming of Ted Lindsay. Terrible Ted was a battler who'd rush into corners where even a Howe would fear to tread. Lindsay used his stick and elbows to carve out a spot in the Hall of Fame. He was tough but he was also talented. Lindsay scored 379 goals in 17 seasons that left his face scarred by more stitches than you'll find on a baseball. Jeremy Roenick is also working on his battle stripes.

ROENICK

In Roenick's first year in the playoffs **ROENICK** five miles! Young Jeremy's NHL the Blackhawks knew this 19 year old schooling had begun.

In Roenick's first year in the playoffs the Blackhawks knew this 19 year old from a prestigious New England prep school was also an honour graduate of hockey's school of hard knocks. With the black curly thread from eight stitches slowly turning into a crusty red because of the blood seeping from a cut he'd taken in the first period, Roenick took another painful blow in the face in the third period. A stick in the mouth left his teeth badly chipped. Roenick shrugged off the pain and, in the stuff that young legends are made of, went out and scored the power-play goal that ignited Chicago. They went on to win the game and the series against St. Louis.

"J.R.'s a borderline superstar right now," says associate coach Darryl Sutter. "He's aggressive. He's a Blackhawk. He's what we want all our players to be. Obviously you won't find that kind of skill all the time, especially combined with that kind of work ethic and love for the game." As Sutter says so succinctly, Roenick is a Blackhawk.

Actually, he was born to be a Red Sox or a Celtic. Hockey has an unending chain of stars, all linked, sometimes by chance, sometimes by coincidence. Chances are if Roenick had been born a few years earlier he would have been like most New England kids and concentrated on baseball or basketball. But a young, exciting defenseman from Owen Sound, Ontario named Bobby Orr had come along to created unprecedented interest in hockey in Boston. Rinks and leagues sprung up everywhere when the big, bad Bruins brought the Stanley Cup back to Boston.

It was coincidence that Roenick first started skating on one of those new rinks and playing in one of those new leagues. The four year old just tagged along with a friend who'd moved recently from Minnesota and didn't want to go to the rink alone. The friend got bored and eventually quit hockey. Roenick was hooked for life. His father's business took the Roenick family all over the eastern seaboard. Their address kept changing but one thing remained constant. Wherever they went little Jeremy played hockey. And he played better than anyone else. Far better. He scored a Gretzky-esque 350 points one season in minor hockey. At twelve they lived in a suburb of Washington, DC and Roenick's shortest road trip was to Philadelphia. His shortest! About one hundred and forty-

five miles! Young Jeremy's NHL schooling had begun.

How far would the Roenicks go to help Jeremy make the NHL? All the way from Washington to New Jersey, every weekend. At 14, Roenick's father Wally would take him to the airport every Friday night. Jeremy would fly on his own to New Jersey to play for a bantam team that was a national champion. After three games in two days, Roenick would fly back home in time for school on Monday. The family put up with that crazy schedule for a year before finally moving back to the Boston area for good...Jeremy's good.

He enrolled in one of the best private schools in Boston mainly because it had one of the best hockey programs in Boston. Roenick quickly made it even better. Thayer Academy won two New England Prep School titles during Roenick's three years in school. Everyone was starting to notice the kid who skated like Denis Savard, worked like Bobby Clarke and scored like Wayne Gretzky. The NHL, however, had been burned once before by overrating a Boston high schooler. Bobby Carpenter was a local legend who eventually would become the first American to score 50 goals in the NHL. But he was a bust for the first couple of years, struggling under the pressure of being the first American taken number one in the NHL draft.

Perhaps because of Carpenter and another American number one flop, Brian Lawton, and maybe because he played too aggressively for his slight build, Roenick wasn't rated that highly by anyone except the Chicago Blackhawks. Their scouts had listed him as the best skater in the entire draft. Coach Mike Keenan also liked his heart and drive. The Blackhawks were thrilled when he was still available when they drafted in eighth position.

Jeremy Roenick had followed the yellow brick road to the NHL. But now he was about to hit a few potholes. He decided to put the NHL on hold and go to college. It didn't take him long to realize his mistake. One week to be exact. After only a week at Boston College he headed north at Wayne Gretzky's urging and played half a season for the Hull, Quebec team that Gretzky owned in the Quebec Junior League. After 70 points in 28 games Roenick had conquered another world and moved on to lead the United States in scoring at the

World Junior Championships. The busiest year of an incredibly busy life was about to get even more hectic. The Blackhawks called him up for the final 20 games of the 1988–'89 season. Roenick's 18 points in 20 NHL games convinced the Blackhawks they had the steal of the draft.

But 26 games into his first full rookie season the Blackhawks were starting to wonder if he was a steal, or was stealing. He wasn't earning his paycheck. With only two goals in 26 games and the worst plus-minus rating on the team, Roenick was feeling guilty every time he cashed a cheque. He was also afraid to answer the telephone. The supportive parents who'd made so many sacrifices for their son were starting to wonder what had gone wrong. The push from his parents that helped get him to the NHL was now a shove—a shove he didn't need.

"Lately I've been hearing a lot from back home about how I'm not playing up to my ability," he told reporters. "That's stuff I don't need right now. I'm looking for positive reinforcements." He got them from an unexpected source. Coach Mike Keenan, the Captain Bligh of hockey, was a demanding, unforgiving coach who drove his crew to the point of exhaustion and mutiny. With Roenick he was uncharacteristically forgiving and fatherly. Driven to distraction, worrying about his mistakes, Roenick had simply lost his confidence. Keenan took him aside and told him to relax and have fun.

There aren't many players who are too intense for their own good. Roenick was obviously one of them. He did relax and he did have great fun for the rest of his rookie year. In his last 54 games he scored 24 goals and had 32 assists for 56 points. He wound up the year with 26 goals, 40 assists and 66 points in his first full season. He finished third in Rookie of the Year balloting behind the Soviet veteran Sergei Makarov and the top

ROENICK

pick in the NHL draft, Mike Modano. In the playoffs, however, the real Roenick emerged. He destroyed the Chicago playoff scoring record of 12 points, scoring 11 goals and setting up 7 others for 18 points in 20 playoff games.

The Blackhawks were relieved and satisfied. They did get the steal of the draft. The best mid-first-round theft since 1979 when Boston got another superstar with the eighth pick, a defenseman named Ray Bourque. Chicago was so happy with Roenick that they traded one of the most productive and exciting players in their history, Denis Savard, to Montreal. They improved their defense

by getting the pugnacious Chris Chelios in return. Chelios provided the maturity but Roenick provided the real leadership and spark for a Blackhawks team that went on to finish first in the regular season. Roenick flirted with his first one-hundred-point season, settling for 41 goals and 54 assists. Everyone else wished someone had shot this J.R. because he also produced ten game-winning goals. The kid had replaced the aging star perfectly. He even had the audacity to steal Savard's best move.

Early in the 1991–'92 season in a game against Toronto, Roenick flashed in over the blueline. The defensemen, worried about Roenick's great speed to the outside, cheated by retreating as quickly as possible. Roenick froze the first defender in his tracks for an instant with a quick drop of the right shoulder and a fake to the inside. Before the defenseman could recover his balance Roenick swirled in a 360 degree circle that drew aahs from the crowd and a curse from the embarrassed defenseman. Realizing his partner was in trouble the other defender came over to help. This guy had no excuse. He'd seen what Roenick had done to his partner. He wouldn't fall for the same move, would he? He did. Another 360 degree spin and Roenick was gone in a blur of red and black. Like victims of a car accident, the defensemen couldn't quite grasp what had happened to them. They stood and watched helplessly as Roenick zipped in and almost with disdain put only half a move on the poor goaltender to finish off the Chicago goal of the year.

That one goal let the rest of the hockey world know what the Blackhawks had realized all along—J.R. was something special. After the game he was almost as embarrassed as the defensemen. He hadn't tried to be flashy. Unlike Savard, he wasn't out to entertain the crowd. He was out to win and he'd do anything it took to do it, even a

ROENICK

circus move. All Roenick wanted to talk about was the hit he'd put on the Leaf's rambunctious Wendell Clark earlier in the game.

The Blackhawks coaching staff is continually amazed that Roenick isn't concerned about goals and assists. His aim each season is to lead the team in takeouts. It's the only statistic he really cares about and the only statistic he checks faithfully after every game.

Darryl Sutter paid him the ultimate compliment when he acknowledged that if the Sutter clan was thinking of adopting another brother, Roenick would be drafted number one. He combines their fiery dedication and tireless work ethic with a desire to be on the ice in every key situation. At 21 he was already telling the veterans what to do and, most amazingly of all, the veterans were listening.

"He's high on life and that's why you never see him have a bad game. He's having so much fun," says Sutter, "that it's not work at all. He likes running into people. He likes people to run into him. The offensive game is just a spin-off. He wants to be better defensively. That says it all about a kid who's a star."

Make that a superstar who, in the 1991–'92 season, got the first of what could be half a dozen straight 50-goal seasons. A superstar who still thinks and plays with the desire of a fourth-line centre trying to hang on to a job. Roenick says, "All I'm trying to do is go out and stir the pot. It gets me going and it gets the team going. I'm not a bad guy. I'm not trying to injure anyone. I just want to frustrate them, provide a spark and get the team going."

The Blackhawks are going back to the future with the throwback—the Blast from the Past—Jeremy Roenick. ★

Joe Sakic

The press releases came regularly to the sports departments of newspapers, radio and television stations in Vancouver during the winter of 1984. They updated the stats to support the growing legend of a Wayne Gretzky of the West Coast, a fifteen year old who could score goals by the hundreds and set them up by the thousands.

SAKIC

Joe Sakic shared something else in common with the godlike Gretzky. Anyone who went to the rink to see what all the fuss was about looked at this skinny waif of a boy and said, "That's what all the fuss is about?" Then, after they'd watched him play, they nodded their heads in belief and came away knowing they'd seen something special. Both Gretzky and Sakic had a talent for squeezing extraordinary performances out of less than ordinary physiques.

Sakic's junior coach summed it up perfectly when he said, "We couldn't believe that the Joe Sakic sitting in the dressing room was the same guy that would go out on the ice. It was like he'd gone

SAKIC

into a phone booth to change or something." It was no phone booth. It was a state of mind he entered that transformed this ordinary Joe into a superboy. "When you play against the best you have to be at your best," says the shy, quiet hero who leads every league in modesty.

His personality and his talent trace back to his hometown. Burnaby is a faceless suburb of Vancouver, a bedroom community famous for producing only one thing—hockey players. A surprisingly long list of NHLers, from the tough Jack McIlhargey to the talented Glenn Anderson and Cliff Ronning to the superstar Joe Sakic. They've all graduated from the Burnaby Minor Hockey Associ-

ation. Its streamlined efficiency and excellent coaching are a couple of reasons why **SAKIC** a community with one of the warmest, wettest climates in Canada can produce nearly a dozen NHLers.

"We had great coaching," says Sakic. "They worked on our skills all the time. While other teams were scrimmaging or working on hitting each other we were practising 3 on 2's or 2 on 1's; the things that help you learn how to handle the puck. It's what every kid should do if he wants to become good."

Another big reason why so many Burnaby kids become good sits tucked away in seclusion just off the Trans Canada highway. The Burnaby Four Rinks arena is exactly what the name says: four rinks where the ice machines and the hockey never stop. It's where the Vancouver Canucks and other NHLers who return home for the summer stay in shape during the off-season. It's where Burnaby kids like Sakic get to be rink rats, squeezing a little extra ice time for themselves and honing the skills that turn a sport into a career. "My friends and I'd go there all the time," says Sakic. "We'd play three or four times a week with our minor hockey teams and then we'd spend every minute or hour we could playing Four Rinks. That's all we did all winter. We didn't do anything else. I just wanted to play hockey and that was it."

Sakic was fortunate that he was never very big. Kids who grow and mature faster than others their age often dominate the game just by throwing their weight, and not the puck, around. They never really learn how to play the game and sooner or later the other kids catch up to them in size. On the rink near his home in Burnaby in those post-midnight hours Joe Sakic, rink rat, skated against players of all ages and developed the puckhandling gifts that would last a lifetime.

Never a super skater, Sakic learned to compensate with quick cutbacks and sprints, using surprise rather than speed to beat defenders. The giants like Lindros and Lemieux use their size and strength. The naturals like Fedorov, Bure and Mogilny use their speed. The creative like Gretzky, Yzerman and Sakic have to use their inventiveness and quickness to control the puck and the game.

Sakic was never an ordinary Joe at any level. In bantam he led the Burnaby Bantam A's to the British Columbia championship and a national title, the Purolator Challenge Cup. "It was the biggest thrill of my life," he recalled. "Seeing your name in the paper was really something when you're a kid. We had a lot of fun but we had to work hard for it." Sakic kept working hard when he moved up to midget and the legendary scoring feats followed. The press releases that flowed were no exaggeration. He was a superstar in midget, and he led B.C. to the national championships. In only 60 games, Sakic scored 86 goals. He added 73 assists for 156 points, a Gretzky-like average of two and a half points per game.

As usual with a player who isn't an overpowering physical specimen, there were doubts that Sakic could play, much less star, in the bigger, faster and certainly rougher world of major junior hockey. He was drafted by Swift Current of the Western Hockey League. Moving from the warmth of the family home in balmy Burnaby to the harsh, cold climate of a small city in Saskatchewan can be a painful transition for a teenager. Not Sakic. It turned out to be a couple of the best years of his life. He shared a common love with the folks of his new hometown. "The people in Swift Current were crazy about hockey." he says. "I loved everything about the place. A couple of teammates and I moved in with this family that made us feel right at home. We had lots of fun. We were a block away from everything—the rink, the school. It was great."

The fun turned to tragedy on an icy prairie highway in mid-season. On December 30th, 1986, the team bus went off the highway, killing four members of the team. Sakic, who was sitting at the front of the bus, was not seriously injured. Physically. Mentally he suffered scars that still make it difficult to discuss what he called the worst thing that ever happened in his life. He still tries to not think about it. The tragedy left a gaping hole in the team. The four victims—Trent Kreese, Scott Kruger, Chris Montoyka and Brent Ruff—were four of the best players on the team. The accident gave Sakic and the rest of the Broncos new incentive. They dedicated the rest of the season to their teammates and wore their numbers in patches on their shoulders. Coach Graham James said, "Joe played like a demon for the rest of the year. Even though he was a rookie he became the leader. He took our team from out of the playoffs to making them comfortably by eleven points."

SAKIC

"I wasn't the rah-rah type in the dressing room," says Sakic. "I just try to work as hard as I can for every game." Leading by example, the 17 year old nearly duplicated his super scoring feats of bantam and midget days. He finished his first year in junior with 60 goals, 73 assists, 133 points. Good, but not great enough to overcome NHL doubts about his size and strength. At 5' 11", 185 pounds he had borderline size. Even worse, NHL scouts feared he was a borderline skater. They projected him as a third- or fourth-line centre at best and a career minor leaguer at worst.

Fourteen players were drafted ahead of him in the 1987 draft, superstars who never were like Pierre Turgeon and celebrated flops who never will be like Wayne McBean and Keith Osborne. Sakic was disappointed but not insulted. He wasn't even Quebec's first choice. They'd taken Bryan Fogarty with their first choice, number nine overall. Fogarty had broken Bobby Orr's scoring records as a defenseman in the Ontario Hockey League, but a drinking problem has so far kept Fogarty from becoming a regular, much less a star, in the NHL.

But Quebec still had their eye on Sakic and were willing to pay a good price to get him. The Nordiques traded the combative Dale Hunter to Washington to get the Caps first round choice. Then, using the 15th pick in the draft, they selected Sakic. Quebec was well aware that number 15 could be the luckiest number in the draft. Another junior scoring sensation considered too sleight and small to survive in the NHL was also chosen fifteenth in his draft year—Hall of Fame, 500 goal scorer Mike Bossy. Like Bossy, Sakic would emerge as the real number one pick of his litter.

The Nordiques were in no rush to push him into the NHL. At 18, he needed one more year of seasoning in junior hockey. He returned to Swift Current to win the WHL scoring title. Actually, he finished in a tie with Moose Jaw's Theoren Fleury at 160 points, but was given the title because he'd scored 78 goals, 10 more than Fleury. He also played for Canada at the World Junior Championship. "That was the first time I played with all the best juniors in the world," says Sakic. "It was a lot faster but I got quite a thrill out of the whole experience. It was great."

The apprenticeship was complete. He was ready for the Nordiques, and they were certainly ready for him. If they needed any references his great rival in junior hockey, Theoren

Fleury, was happy to supply them. "Joe was as good as they come in the Western League. He's a natural goalscorer and a great playmaker." Fleury added the greatest compliment one small guy can give another, "Joe doesn't back down from the rough stuff."

Sakic moved into the NHL as smoothly and effortlessly as he'd moved up to every other step on the hockey ladder. He scored his first goal in his second game in the NHL, beating New Jersey's Sean Burke. Early in December he played the most expensive game in his life. He had to buy a dozen tickets for family and friends in Burnaby when he returned home to play in Vancouver for the first

SAKIC

time. "It was strange," he recalls. "I was a Canuck fan when I grew up and suddenly I was playing against them. It felt really weird."

Throughout his career trips to Vancouver would always bring out the best in him. He played some of his best games against the Canucks, twice beating them singlehandedly with late goals including one brilliant solo effort in overtime. His first trip to Vancouver wasn't his best as he was slowed by an ankle injury that lowered his rookie production. But everyone could see the potential, including a superstar Sakic would soon replace. Peter Stastny, arguably the greatest and certainly the most productive European to ever play in the NHL, became

an instant fan of the skinny kid from Burnaby. "His moves in practice and in games, they're incredible," gushed Stastny. "Right now he tries too hard and when he learns to relax he'll be great. He posesses all those talents, all those skills that are needed for a great hockey player."

Stastny thought the ankle wasn't the only thing slowing the rookie's start. "Suddenly he's got huge headlines," he said. "He's on the front page of all the papers in Quebec. Like it or not the pressure is there." Sakic chuckles that actually it wasn't: "Whatever they wrote in the papers I couldn't understand anyway because I don't speak French. So there wasn't any pressure on me at all." Some players find Quebec City almost a foreign country because of the language. Sakic never had anything beyond grade eleven French and made no effort to learn the language. He found he could always get by, "Everybody speaks too fast for me so it wouldn't have done me any good to take lessons. But almost everyone speaks English too so they help you out."

He got great help from one French-speaking

SAKIC

Quebecker in his second year. After a 62-point rookie season, in his second year Sakic blossomed into the star Quebec so desperately needed. The potential that Peter Stastny had recognized began to emerge. Sakic exploded for the first of two straight 100-point seasons. He played in his first All Star game thanks to the help and sportsmanship of Quebec-born Hall of Famer Guy Lafleur. Lafleur was named to the All Star team on reputation alone. He didn't feel he deserved to be there but he knew who did—Joe Sakic.

"I passed the invitation over to Joe," says Lafleur. "He was the Nordiques best player at the time and definitely deserved to be in Pittsburgh (site of the 1989 All Star game). The kid is going to be a star in this league." Two superstars can't be wrong. Sakic made Lafleur and Peter Stastny look like Hall of Fame forecasters by developing into the centre of attention in Quebec City. The Nordiques traded Stastny to New Jersey and started stockpiling draft choices, rebuilding a fallen franchise around this extra-ordinary Joe from Burnaby. ★

Brendan Shanahan

It's late in Brendan Shanahan's fifth season in the NHL. It's been his most difficult year since his rookie season in 1987–'88. His teammate Brett Hull is on his way to another 80-goal season. Craig Janney is the new centre of attention in every sense of the word after coming over from Boston in a controversial late-season trade for Adam Oates, the man Hull called the best player he's ever played with. For the moment, the stars are ignored by a pack of reporters huddled around Shanahan—the living definition of a solid, hard-working, two-way winger. "Hey Shannie," hollered a teammate amused by all the attention being paid to Shanahan. "What'd you do, rob a bank this weekend?" "No," replied a sheepish Shanahan, "But guess which name I've heard a hundred times this interview?"

It's the name that won't go away. The name he's heard a thousand times in a thousand interviews all winter long. The name that may be forever linked with his own: Abbott and Costello, Rowan and Martin, Thelma and Louise, Siskel and Ebert, Shanahan and Stevens. The name was Scott Stevens. He was the defensive building block St. Louis had acquired at extravagant cost the year before. He was supposed to be the foundation for a string of Stanley Cup successes. Instead, Scott Stevens became the price the Blues had to pay to get Brendan Shanahan. They gambled and lost.

SHANAHAN

In July, 1991, St. Louis signed Shanahan, a highly-publicized free **SHANAHAN** agent who'd taken a big gamble of his own when he played out his contract with New Jersey, the team that had chosen him second overall in the '87 draft. He had all the right numbers, the statistical parameters a computer would spit out if you asked it to define the perfect NHL winger. 6' 3". 215 pounds. 29 goals, 37 assists, 66 points, 141 minutes in penalties. The numbers added up to a four-year, five million-dollar contract with the Blues.

St. Louis couldn't resist the temptation to take one of the best young wingers in the game, even though they knew they'd have to compensate New Jersey heavily for the loss of a type one free agent. General Manager Ron Caron was willing to give up forward Rod Brind'amour, goalie Curtis Joseph plus two draft picks. Satisfied that even if he lost he'd be well compensated, New Jersey General Manager Lou Lamoriello decided to ask for the moon. He chose Scott Stevens, an NHL all-star who was unquestionably one of the top five defensemen in the league.

The NHL arbitrator had to decide between one proposal and the other. He was not allowed to try to work out a compromise. He shocked everyone, even Lamoriello, by giving the Devils Scott Stevens. Shanahan's heart sank when he heard the news. First he had the pressure of proving he was worth all the money. Now he had to prove he was worth an even bigger price, Scott Stevens. "Fortunately there wasn't any resentment toward me when I arrived," he said. "The resentment was toward the arbitrator who made the ruling. The fans in St. Louis have been great. They were very generous to me from the moment I got here."

Fortunately for Shanahan he'd also been through it all before. Nothing could have been worse than the despair and loneliness of his NHL rookie season. "There's always a bit of confidence you haven't gained yet," he remembers. "That's how I felt my first year. It took me a long time to gain confidence in myself."

The agony of that first season, in which he scored only 7 goals, was the only sad chapter in the storybook life of Brendan Shanahan. Growing up in suburban Toronto, he could skate from the time he learned to walk. "It wasn't my parents, it was my three older brothers that got me started," he says. They all played house league hockey. Every weekend the boys would pack up their gear and their baby brother and head for the rink at 7 A.M. Brendan affectionately remembers the wonder years of his life. "I loved it," he says. "The hockey rink was a playground for me as a toddler."

While his brothers played on the ice, little Brendan would noisily run around the halls with a broken stick, a puck fashioned out of rolled-up tape, and play imaginary games with legendary linemates. "I was Darryl Sittler's winger. I bumped Errol Thompson off the line. Darryl, Lanny and I would pass that tape around the halls for hours. I'd always score the game-winner." Twenty years later a boyish excitement comes over him as he recalls the sweet memories of his enchanted childhood. His dreams did come true, with one notable exception. "I've never scored an overtime goal in the NHL," he says. "And I only did it once in junior."

The rest of his life did come eerily close to those childhood dreams. In the 1991 Canada Cup, Shanahan found himself on a breakout with a legend and for a second he wasn't sure if it was reality or a dream. "I had a two-on-one with Gretzky," he

laughingly recalls. "I gave him the **SHANAHAN** you spend long hours on the phone puck right away. I said, 'you carry the mail.' He did, and then slid me a perfect pass. I one-timed it into a nearly-empty net. I laughed after that because I'd imagined it so many times when I was a kid. It was hard to believe I was there and actually doing it. It makes you shake your head. To the fans in the stands you're just another player, but it's incredible to be on the ice with people you idolize."

Even though Darryl Sittler was his first hockey hero, Brendan Shanahan didn't model his game after any one player. He tried to learn a little something from everyone he played with or against. He studied how Brett Hull managed to sneak into position to score goals that looked ridiculously easy to the untrained eye. New Jersey linemate Kirk Muller, the one player he's most often compared to, taught him how to become one of the best boardmen in the business. He showed him a clever little move to gain time in the corners. "You step on the puck," he explains, "that way no one can take it away from you while you try to find someone to pass it to. A small thing, but if you're receptive to all the little things they can add up to making you a little better player every year."

Always big for his age, Brendan Shanahan convinced his parents to let him start his competitive career before he'd even reached the age of five. The precociousness and early maturity were chacteristics that marked his career at every step. At 16 he scored 28 goals for London in the rugged Ontario Hockey League. The next year he scored 39 times and came within 8 points of a 100-point season. He also had enough penalty minutes to prove his toughness. The scouts unanimously agreed. He was the second-best player in the draft, right behind "the next Mario Lemieux" of the Quebec league, Pierre Turgeon. New Jersey regarded Shanahan as a stronger, all-around player and gladly took him with the second pick.

The size and maturity that had helped him play with older kids throughout his childhood fooled the Devils into thinking that he was one of the few 18 year olds capable of stepping directly into the NHL. He did, but not without a lot of misery. "I wasn't ready, physically or emotionally. I had to grow up in the NHL," he says. "I came close to losing my confidence. There were low points when

you spend long hours on the phone back home." Shanahan was lost, struggling on the ice, racked by homesickness off the ice. "I couldn't associate with my teammates. I was too young. They were too old. I remember my first trip to Toronto. They were going out to dinner, I was sneaking out the back door to go to a high school dance. My buddies were all in the senior year in high school. I'd rather hang around with them than with 26- or 27-year-old family men. I didn't understand them. They didn't understand me. It seemed like there were centuries between us."

The time gap started to narrow in the playoffs. After a disappointing 7 goal, 26 point rookie season, Shanahan relaxed and started bashing and crashing bodies in the playoffs. "For the first time I started to feel part of the team," he recalls. "I proved that if I was too slow afoot or too slow reading the play I could still help out with the physical side, fighting as much as I could." Novelists would describe it as finally finding your voice. Shanahan had finally found the blend of toughness and finesse that would make him one of the best young wingers in the league. He scored twice and had 44 rambunctious penalty minutes in a dozen playoff games at the end of his rookie year.

The next season he continued to rock 'em and sock 'em. For the next three years he'd average 27 goals, 36 assists, 63 points and 131 minutes in penalties. After scoring 30 goals in his third year Shanahan decided to play out his option and test his value on the free agent market. St. Louis Coach Brian Sutter looked at Shanahan and saw a mirror-image of himself. Sutter says, "He's a big strong kid with real soft hands. He handles the puck very well in traffic. He's outstanding along the boards."

A year later the Blues still miss Scott Stevens but they're happy with Shanahan. He gave them the second-line strength they needed to take the pressure and close-checking away from the Hull line. He bought a summer home in Ireland to get away from the game and get back to his roots. The luck of the Irish stays with Brendan Shanahan. "Playing the sport I'm playing and making a living at it makes you realize how privileged we are. So many people go through life working at jobs they can't stand. I enjoy showing up for work every day. I'm very lucky and very grateful." ★

Mats Sundin

Graceful and elegant are words the NHL thought they had retired with Jean Beliveau. There aren't many players with that rare combination of style and fluidity. The 6' 3" Beliveau seemed to glide in slow motion before using his remarkable reach to slide the puck effortlessly past a confused goaltender, who never knew until the last second whether Beliveau was going to his backhand or forehand.

Since those days of the original six, the game has come a long way in short, choppy strides. Today hockey is quickness and strength. Hooking and holding have become the great equalizers, slowing down the gifted and skilled players. It's created a homogenous blend of talent that makes scrappy, marginally-talented players like the Hunter and Sutter brothers nearly as valuable as the stars of the league.

SUNDIN

It's not often you see a player who **SUNDIN** tial. He was easily the best skater in the combines the best of both eras. Mats draft. And he had the perfect size and Sundin also combines the best of both modern attitude. But he also had military and hockey com- styles of hockey, European and North American. mitments to fulfill in Sweden.

His long, lanky body—6' 2", 190 pounds—makes him a near-perfect clone of Beliveau. It makes him a smooth, natural skater, as fluid as Beliveau but even quicker. His early exposure to international hockey made him one of the few Europeans with a North American attitude.

A month before the draft Djurgarden—another team in the Swedish Elite League—had pressured the teenager into agreeing to a new contract. He'd resisted at first but finally he reluctantly signed the new deal in a parking lot, without the help of an agent or adviser. Sundin had no idea that his mar- ket value would soar dramatically a month later in North America. That spring, his play in the World Junior Championships had moved him up quickly in the scouting reports. The official scouting line

The Swedish stereotype was established decades ago when that crusty curmudgeon, Harold Ballard, uttered one of the most famous put-downs in the history of hockey. He complained that Inge Ham- marstrom, the Swedish winger Punch Imlach had signed against Ballard's wishes, could go into a corner with eggs in his pockets and come out without breaking them. Times and Swedes change. Sundin could go into a corner with those same eggs and come out with the puck, leaving a defenseman with omelet all over his face. Like his fellow Swede, Tomas Sandstrom, Sundin is a devout believ- er in the rule of the NHL jungle—an elbow for an elbow, a high stick for a high stick.

Scouts who watched the teenager grow up in his native Stockholm were surprised at his feistiness. It seemed so incongruous to see that kind of chip- piness coming from someone so tal- ented, so innocent and boyish looking. The baby-face Nelson of Swedish hockey was a good but not great player in the Swedish Elite League. At 17 he made his debut with Nacka, scoring ten goals in 25 games; hardly the statistical sign of a super- star. But his natural ability and super skating moved him near the top of all scouting lists in a year when the pool of junior talent was very shallow.

The Quebec Nordiques, who need- ed immediate help, shocked everyone in 1989 by making Sundin the first player chosen in the draft. There was no question he had the most poten-

on him was "a power forward with a scoring touch who reads the game well and is an excellent skater."

SUNDIN

The Nordiques, who were building for the future, didn't see anyone in the draft that could help them enough in the short term to make it worthwhile to pass on Sundin, so they happily made him number one. And because they didn't think he was ready to step into the NHL immediately anyway, they didn't mind waiting for him. Fans in Quebec City and elsewhere around the NHL shook their heads in disbelief that the Nordiques could afford to waste a pick on a virtual unknown who was years away from playing in the NHL, and might never even come to North America.

Despite the cynicism, however, everyone was immediately impressed by Sundin's appearance and deportment at the draft in Minneapolis. He was not only big he was also very mature, despite his youthful face. He was the calm in the middle of the media hurricane, casually stickhandling around difficult questions with near-perfect English. The Nordiques watched with growing satisfaction, knowing they had a confident young man who had a firm hold on reality and his destiny.

He returned home to honor his obligation with Djurgarden but Quebec had planted the seeds of doubt and disenchantment. He realized he'd made a mistake. He began a long, ugly battle to get out of it. To this day he calls it the worst period of his life. "I was very disappointed with the whole situation," he recalls bitterly. "Everyone criticized me. The Swedish media called me all kinds of names and made my family feel very poorly. I was very upset with the people on the Djurgarden team. They gave me no respect. They threatened to ban me from international hockey for life if I left. I felt bad about it."

But Sundin wasn't banned. He played out the year in Sweden, helping Swedish teams do well at the world and world junior championships. He still had three years left on his four-year contract but, he says, "I was steamed with Djurgarden." Mad enough to leave the increasingly messy situation behind him and get away to Quebec that September, leaving an agent and the Nordiques president, Marcel Aubut, behind in Sweden to work out a settlement with his old club. The lawyer for Djurgarden knew the contract Sundin had signed in the parking lot wasn't a legal and binding document. They could stall Sundin's departure to the NHL, but they knew they could never stop it. The Swedish team happily agreed to settle for money instead. The Nordiques bought out his contract for $350,000 and quickly signed him to a five-year deal that averaged out to nearly $300,000 per season.

Any questions about Sundin being worth all the trouble and expense quickly disappeared. He'd grown up idolizing Swedish stars Kent Nillson—one of the slickest stickhandlers and passers in hockey, and Mats Naslund—the exciting little buzzbomb. Quebec fans saw a little of each in Sundin. They also saw a hint of the second coming of Jean Beliveau, who'd starred with the Quebec Aces forty years before.

In his first exhibition game a near-sellout crowd gave Sundin a standing ovation after a breathtaking end-to-end rush. Sundin was thrilled by the warm welcome. "I'd like to thank everyone for their patience," he said. "I'm convinced I made the right decision (to come to Quebec). The coaches are great with the kids and I know I'm going to learn a lot more here." Aubut breathed a huge sigh of relief and said, "We all got what we wanted. We succeeded in not only signing him but also guaranteed that Mats will be able to represent his country in international play."

The Nordiques wanted to ease Sundin into the NHL but he made it difficult. Even at 19 he was too big, too fast and too good to sit on the bench. He scored a goal and set up three others in his second pre-season game. "I couldn't believe how fast it was; a lot faster than the best league in Sweden and a lot rougher too." But he still loved it, adding "It's a dream come true for me."

It was the fulfillment of a bigger dream for Quebec. They had the top choice in the 1990 draft as well. But that pick, Owen Nolan, would suffer through an agonizing rookie season, scoring only three goals. Sundin's arrival eased the embarrassment and eased the pressure on both Nolan and the Nordiques. No one was happier with Sundin than his coach Dave Chambers, "He's so big and strong and he has the long reach of a Beliveau or Lemieux," he gushed. "You combine that with his intelligence, desire and skill and you have quite an extraordinary player."

Unlike a lot of newcomers to Quebec City, the worldly Sundin had little trouble adjusting to life away from the rink in the French citadel. And on the ice, the adjustment was becoming easier than he expected. "I'm impressed by the intensity level," he told reporters midway through his rookie season. "Most of the games here are as tight as a final game in a world championship. It's quicker and tougher because the rinks are smaller." He was especially impressed by the way NHL stars like Guy Lafleur and Joe Sakic went out of their way to help him adjust. His first year was as smooth as his skating. He scored 23 goals and wound up second in team scoring with 59 points. His only regret was the losing attitude he found in the Quebec dressing room. "There were half a dozen guys who were poisoning the whole atmosphere because they didn't want to play here. They wouldn't work very hard and that had a negative influence on the younger players." Sundin's outspokenness caught the attention of Quebec management. Pierre Page was well aware of the problem and quickly unloaded the malcontents. The soft-spoken Swede had established himself as a team leader.

There wasn't much time off in the off-season for Sundin. After Quebec missed the playoffs he returned to help Sweden win the World Championship in 1991 in Finland. He had a couple of months to recover in Sweden and then it was back on the ice in mid-summer to prepare for the Canada Cup. Number 13 was number one for Sweden. He led the Swedes into the semi-final against Canada. They lost to the eventual champion but Sundin was brilliant. He was named to the All-Tournament team but was still disappointed. "It was a wonderful experience proving to my countrymen that I hadn't made a mistake by going to the NHL, but we were inconsistent. Some good games, some bad. If we'd played the way we played at the World Championship we could have won it all."

After the high of the Canada Cup came the low of another long, losing season in Quebec. The Nordiques were the first team in NHL history to have the first choice in the draft three years in a

SUNDIN

row. They'd taken Sundin, Nolan and Eric Lindros. But Lindros had refused to even talk about playing in Quebec City. The Lindros controversy hung over Quebec all season. They got off to a miserable start and it got even worse. Sundin was worn out after two training camps, a World Championship, a Canada Cup, and a grueling NHL season in only twelve months. "I felt invincible," he explains. "I thought I could do it all, but I couldn't."

He was invisible for most of the first half of the 1991–'92 season, playing poorly, without heart or energy. A perplexed Page had fired Chambers and taken over as coach himself. In desperation, after losing Sakic to injury, he moved Sundin from right wing to centre in mid-season. After playing the position in Sweden, Sundin looked and felt right at home in the middle. "I have a lot more room to manoeuver," he said, "And I have the puck a lot more."

And he did a lot more with it. In nearly 60 games at right wing he'd scored just 15 goals. In 21 games at centre, he produced 17 goals. Late in the year he saved the Nordiques from record-setting embarrassment. They were threatening to become the first team in NHL history to go an entire season without winning a single game on the road. Sundin saved them from ignominy with a phenomenal game in Hartford in early March. He scored five times to break the team single game record held by super-scorers Peter Stastny and Michel Goulet. He also helped new linemates Valeri Kamensky and Owen Nolan score three more.

Sundin, the master of understatement, said "Our line was really clicking. The whole team was pumped. It's a big relief. We have to keep going and build on it." They didn't. Only the expansion San Jose Sharks saved the Nordiques from finishing dead last in the league for a fourth straight season.

The past and present were dismal, but the future finally looked better with Sundin ready to deliver. "Those 100-point seasons will come," he said. "I hope to be here a long time. I want to be here when we finally turn things around." ★

About the Author

Eric Dwyer remembers when Jean Beliveau was one of hockey's young superstars. He got hooked on hockey as a child in Montreal in the 1950s when Beliveau and Rocket Richard were leading the Canadiens to five Stanley Cups in a row. Hockey has remained a lifelong love affair. The former newsman and radio talk show host has worked as a sportscaster for CBC Radio and TV in Vancouver since 1980. He's covered the Summer and Winter Olympics, the Commonwealth Games, the U.S. Open at Pebble Beach, The Canadian Open of Tennis, and thousands of football, hockey, baseball and soccer games. But the biggest thrill of his sportscasting career was covering the miracle of '82—the Vancouver Canucks' exciting and unexpected drive to the Stanley Cup Finals in 1982. This is his first book.